The Teenage Guide to Life Online

**To the many wonderful friends I simply wouldn't have
if not for the Internet and social media.
You know who you are.**

All the advice in this book is given in good faith and after a great deal
of care and consideration. However, every situation is different
and sometimes effective and safe advice requires specific knowledge
of that situation. If you have any doubts or if your situation seems
different from those described here, please always seek help
from a trusted adult such as a teacher, professional or other
person who cares about you.

First published 2018 by Walker Books Ltd
87 Vauxhall Walk, London SE11 5HJ

2 4 6 8 10 9 7 5 3 1

Text © 2018 Nicola Morgan

The right of Nicola Morgan to be identified as author of this work has been
asserted by her in accordance with the Copyright, Designs and Patents Act 1988

This book has been typeset in Clarendon and Shinn

Printed and bound by CPI Group (UK) Ltd, Croydon CR0 4YY

British Library Cataloguing in Publication Data:
a catalogue record for this book is available from the British Library

ISBN: 978-1-4063-7790-3

www.walker.co.uk

NICOLA MORGAN

The Teenage Guide to Life Online

WALKER BOOKS
AND SUBSIDIARIES

LONDON · BOSTON · SYDNEY · AUCKLAND

Contents

Introduction

Only a few years ago, the phrase "life online" wouldn't have made sense. In some places and societies around the world and for certain groups of people everywhere, it *still* doesn't. But for most of us, "life online" is just how things are nowadays. You probably take it for granted that you can look anything up really quickly, contact your friends instantly, talk to people on the other side of the world, get news incredibly fast, ask for support, connect to a group of people with the same problem, find out what your homework is, buy things without leaving home, play a game with someone thousands of miles away, watch a video about almost anything you can imagine. The opportunities and advantages are enormous.

The Internet and the World Wide Web (I'll explain the difference later) have vastly changed our lives and how we spend our days – and nights. This new online life is changing *us*, too: changing our brains, but only because *everything* we do changes our brains, sometimes positively, sometimes negatively, sometimes both or neither. Every choice we make, everything we spend time on and especially things we spend a lot of time on alter our brains and minds. And we are, many of us, spending a *lot* of time online!

As well as the huge benefits, there are dangers and downsides. Because all this is new, we are only just starting to see what the negatives might be. Many people are worried, and some are very worried. But are we right to be worried and, if so, how worried should we be? Of course, we can't yet know what the long-term effects might be, because we haven't been using the Internet for long enough, but we're going to need to keep a watchful eye on the science so that we can take steps to live well online and have all the benefits without the possible problems. This book aims to sort through the science and bring you the truth as far as we know it. It also aims to make you think about far more than simple online safety, which you will have learnt at school and home already.

One important point: this is not just about young people. What I'm going to show you and share with you is equally true for your parents and teachers. This book may be called a *teenage* guide, but in fact it's for everyone. So I hope you will take the chance to educate your adults as to why they, too, would benefit from being in control of their smartphone and screen use; why switching off their devices an hour or two before bed will help them sleep; why people of all ages are biologically drawn towards social media and checking how many "likes" their latest post received; that their mental health can also be affected by Internet use; and that their brains are likely to be affected in many of the same ways as yours.

Parents shouldn't fear the Internet but they should be informed. So, inform them!

The Teenage Guide to Life Online reveals the facts, ideas and fascinating science behind what happens to us all when we spend time online. The mind-expanding advantages and the mind-shrinking risks. Because when we understand the risks, the psychological and scientific reasons why we are all vulnerable to them, only then can we avoid the negatives, be strong and remain human in a digital world. This book is about what the Internet does to our lives; how it entices and persuades us; and, crucially, how it distracts us. If we want to work well, be healthy and have the best life possible – online and offline – we have to know this. And it's fascinating, too, because it's about us and our behaviours and emotions.

We all need to understand how this wonderful World Wide Web affects us, so that it remains a tool and not a tyrant. This books sets out to explore and compare the positives and the negatives. We can have all the positives and avoid the negatives. We can have control. And we need to, for our own well-being and success.

Welcome to the Internet

A Brief History

The Internet began in the 1960s. But the World Wide Web – WWW or often just called the Web – was invented in 1989. People tend to talk about the Internet when they really mean the Web, and I sometimes do the same.

But let me clarify the difference anyway.

The Internet is *hardware.* It is the network of connected computers and devices all around the world. Any gadget you use to connect to websites – a computer, tablet or smartphone, for example – is part of the Internet when it is connected (including if connected wirelessly).

There is disagreement about how the Internet began, who began it and why. The most common theory is that it was started in 1969 by the US military, who wanted a way to communicate if there was a war or any reason they couldn't send messages by phone. Later, universities started using it to communicate between themselves, too. But the sort of messages and information-sharing that could happen would have looked very different from what we see on our screens today. Much more basic.

The World Wide Web is the *content*: the information and software which we access and use with our Internet-connected devices. The information has to be coded so that it can be read by different operating systems (OS) and using different browsers or software. In the early days, there were different computer languages, and you could only communicate with other computers that used the same language. In theory, that's still the case, but the two main systems – Windows and Apple's iOS – are sufficiently compatible that you can communicate even if you have a different OS from your friend.

The Web was invented by British computer scientist Sir Tim Berners-Lee, who was responsible for developing "HTTP", the language system in which text can be coded in order to be shared between computers. Using this, in 1989 Berners-Lee sent the first successful HTTP communication between a computer and a server. From then on, any computers connected to that server could send and receive data.

How Big Is It?

It's hard to measure the Web, partly because it's so huge, partly because a lot of it is invisible and partly because it's growing all the time. And websites die, but we can't always be sure they are dead. You know when you click a link and it says "page not found"? Well, that content might still be there but the link is broken, or it and the site it was on might have been deleted.

Here are some ways in which we can try to measure the Internet or the Web.

HOW MANY PEOPLE USE THE INTERNET?

We can count the number of homes with a connection, but we can't know how many people are connected to the Internet in any one home. After all, two people might share an account, or younger people might not have their own account. There are also people who use public connections in libraries, for example, or who may just access the Internet on their phone, and they will not be included in these figures.

For a fascinating insight into how fast the overall figure is changing, visit the site Internet Live Stats. You'll see the number changing in front of your eyes!

From that site when I looked in 2018: "Around 40% of the world population has an internet connection today. In 1995, it was less than 1%. The number of internet users has increased tenfold from 1999 to 2013. The first billion was reached in 2005. The second billion in 2010. The third billion in 2014."

Notice that the first billion took six years, the second billion took five and the third took four.

The number of devices connected to the Internet is estimated to reach three times the global population by 2021.

HOW MANY WEBSITES?

Estimates say that we topped a billion at some point in 2016, making over 65 billion web pages.

Another way of looking at it is this, from an article in *The Atlantic* in 2015: "In 1994 there were fewer than 3,000 websites online. By 2014, there were more than 1 billion. That represents a 33 million percent increase in 20 years."

HOW MUCH INFORMATION?

Well, you have already got a sense of how many websites and pages there might be. But the information that is out there, available for you to access if you want to, is vast. There isn't really a word for its vastness!

Daniel J. Levitin, in *The Organized Mind*, says: "Each of us has the equivalent of over half a million books stored on our computers... We have created a world with 300 exabytes (300,000,000,000,000,000,000 pieces) of human-made information. If each of those pieces of information were written on a 3 x 5 index card and then spread out side by side, just one person's share – *your* share of this information – would cover every square inch of Massachusetts and Connecticut combined."

Research conducted in September 2016 by Statistic Brain showed that 1,325,000,000 people were using YouTube; 300 hours of content were being uploaded per minute; 4,950,000,000 videos were viewed per day; and over 10,000 videos had been seen over a billion times.

You can read more statistics and figures on StatisticBrain's "YouTube Company Statistics" web page.

An April 2016 MyGaming report estimated that "The amount of gamers in the world has reached 1.8 billion." Since there were only about 7.4 billion people alive in 2016, we can conclude that gaming is something that over a quarter of people apparently do – and the world population includes tiny babies and small children, who don't play. According to the same report, just over a quarter of gamers in 2016 were under eighteen, and slightly more were male than female (56% versus 44%).

Then there is the Internet of Things – IoT. This describes all the other gadgets we increasingly have that are connected to the Internet and can send and receive data and be controlled remotely, from a smartphone, for example. Many domestic fridges, burglar alarm systems, watches, heating or household electrical items and cars are part of the IoT and this number is growing all the time.

You can buy a fridge that tells you when you've run out of milk or whatever and which can even order your milk for you online. The last thing I want is my fridge making decisions for me but I know lots of people do. I know someone who has a cat-cam, so she can watch her cat when she's at work – and even play with it by making light dance around the room. Considering I'm cautious about aspects of this, it's interesting that between starting to write this book and doing the final version, I've acquired devices to control my heating and some lights when I'm away from home.

More seriously, medical devices can be connected: a doctor in Cambridge, Massachusetts, can take a look at your scan or x-ray while you're in hospital in Cambridge, United Kingdom. In December 2016, *Business Insider* predicted that by 2020, 24 billion things would be connected to the IoT, which is about four devices for every human on the planet. Including babies – and indeed baby monitors are already connected to the IoT.

Call it the Internet or the Web, this thing is huuuuuuuge! It's growing and changing all the time and most of those figures will probably have changed enormously by the time you are reading this. No wonder we are both excited and a little bit scared of it all. No wonder, too, that some people, including perhaps your parents, grandparents and teachers, think of it as a monster. It's certainly a giant and capable of great harm when approached carelessly, but giants can be friendly, too. We can learn to tame them so they work on our side. And this is exactly what we need to do: not run away from the Internet or hide from it but understand it, use it and make it work for us.

How Smartphones Changed Everything

The word "smartphone" was first used in 1995, although the gadget itself was invented three years earlier. Previously, we had simple mobile phones, which could make calls and text, and various devices called PDAs (Personal Digital Assistants) which had very basic functions such as diaries, note-taking and address books. These were pretty much only used by employees to communicate with their office when they were out, and there was virtually no social use. There were incompatible operating systems and the devices were expensive to buy and to operate, so it was hard to justify buying one yourself. And there wasn't much non-work stuff you could do anyway, just the most basic games and nothing you could call social media.

But in 2007 this all changed with the advent of Apple's first iPhone. Steve Jobs, the Apple boss, called it a "revolutionary and magical product". Soon Google launched the Android operating system, and ever since, Apple, Google, Microsoft and Samsung have been competing for either the most popular operating system or the bestselling devices. Various other companies have fallen by the wayside, victims of huge competition.

According to the website Statista, in 2014 there were 1.57 billion smartphone users around the world. This is predicted to rise to 2.87 billion by 2020.

Worldwide sales of new smartphones (according to Statista) were as follows:

2007   122.3 million
2010   296 million
2014   1,244 million (1.24 billion)
2016   1,495 million (1.49 billion)

According to the Statista website, around 10% of the world population used a smartphone in 2011 and this is predicted to rise to 37% in 2020, more than tripling in ten years.

The stats for smartphone use in countries such as the US and UK show that we really do love our little devices. The various studies I've seen – such as research by the UK's Ofcom in 2015 and the well-known Generation Z report by Wikia in 2013 – suggest that users probably spend on average nearly two hours a day online via their smartphones and check their device around fifty times a day. Over a third of people check their smartphone within five minutes of waking up, with those aged between eighteen and twenty-four doing this much more than older adults, at nearly 50%.

These figures may have changed somewhat since those studies were done, as this is a world that is changing fast. On the other hand, we should not assume that increases will continue or at the same speed. Just because there have been huge increases in use over the last decade shouldn't make us assume the same changes will happen in the next ten. People might start to use devices less or at least stop increasing usage so quickly.

Clearly, many of us are spending our time differently from how people did before and we know that how we spend our time alters how our brains are "wired" – which can be good or bad. We will need to think carefully about which changes we are happy about and which we might not be.

So, although the Internet and World Wide Web were massive life-changers for millions and then billions of people, it's that little device that so many of us have in our pockets, constantly close to us, ready to pick up and use at a moment's notice, that has *really* changed lives. You've grown up with it but your parents and teachers have had to learn fast. Some of us have done a good job and some of us not so much.

THE WEB AND YOUNG PEOPLE

Ever since ordinary people and families had access to the Internet and began to read and contribute to information on the Web, adults have worried about some of the risks for young people. Worries include safety, false information, effects on mental states and schoolwork, and access to material that could harm or disturb your mind. And so, along came parental controls and various ways that responsible adults try to make sure that your interaction with the Web is as safe and positive as possible. Adults are only at the start of getting to grips with this.

Trouble is, controlling use is difficult, for several reasons.

1. The Web is so vast and so fast-changing that it's very difficult to keep it safe. Bad people and dangerous sites will find a way through protective measures.
2. It's human nature that when someone says we can't have or do something, many of us try to find a way to have or do exactly that. And this is likely to be very true of young people. Also, young people are often more tech-savvy than their parents, so finding a way to get around rules is easy for them!
3. The stats do seem to show that young people (13–18 and 18–24) use smartphones and other devices on average more than people who are older (though many people in their 30s to 50s are also keen, heavy and expert users). So if overuse *can* cause problems, young people may well be affected more than others.
4. For reasons you'll soon discover, using our devices and accessing social media are activities that are enormously tempting – even addictively so. The biology of this is fascinating and something we need to understand.
5. Too many adults don't yet know enough about all this. Sometimes they are afraid of the wrong things. Often they use the wrong methods to control your Internet or screen use.

6. Very often, adults set an extremely bad example. I will talk about that a lot more in this book. Adults and teenagers should follow the same rules for the same reasons.

I am not here to be bossy and put up barriers or say you shouldn't do this or that. I'm here to try to find the truth and to share it, to be balanced, honest, interesting and to help you, your friends and family to find ways to live well online.

In a way, we are all like teenagers in this new world. We are all quite new to it, finding our way, learning how to manage this hyperconnected way of living. The etiquette, behaviours, healthy messages: they are all at early stages. We haven't got it right yet.

What we are starting to realize – and people of all ages will recognize this equally – is just how incredibly tempting our devices are. (The next section explains why.) If you think you are addicted to yours – or if your parents think you are – you should see me struggle to meet a deadline while allowing myself to be distracted by the various social media platforms I engage with. It's not a pretty sight! I am constantly trying to improve my online use, so that I get my work done brilliantly *and* have a healthy time.

In a way, I'm writing this book for me and for you. I want to live well online and, for that, I need to be clear about the truth.

Let's go and find it.

Why Is It All So Tempting?

I think it's really important and also empowering to understand just why our screens are so tempting. Even addictive. The word "addictive" is not an exaggeration, as you'll see, though being addicted to tech is *not the same* as being dependent on drugs or alcohol: it uses similar brain processes but all the various things we can be addicted to bring different problems.

Make sure your parents and teachers don't skip this section! They need to know, for two reasons. First, so they can understand why you may find it hard to put your phone down; and second, so they can recognize and manage their own habits.

It all comes down to biology again: how humans are programmed in order to survive, grow stronger and succeed. The first things we need for survival are food, shelter and safety; but once we have those, there are other behaviours and activities that will help us succeed, as individuals and as a species. Our biology makes us do these things by rewarding us with a feeling of pleasure or excitement.

There are three particular behaviours which will really help us understand just why the Internet and social media are so attractive and tempting. We are programmed to be:

1. **Social** – We are drawn towards making connections with other people, whether as close friends,

acquaintances, peers or just the people you know in your community: teachers, school caretakers or kitchen staff, school bus drivers, librarians, shopkeepers, the person who helps you cross the street. We may have families, colleagues, friends or partners. We make connections of various sorts between them all and those connections are useful. In evolutionary terms, being social helps us survive and be successful. Humans would not be so successful without our ability to live and work together, to get help from each other, sharing burdens and knowledge.

2. **Curious** – We are drawn towards discovering things, trying things, understanding new things. We *like* to know stuff. We get pleasure from investigating things to see if we might enjoy them and if they might be useful to us. In evolutionary terms, being curious helps us be successful. The more we know, the stronger we can be, the more we can achieve. Being curious also has risks, but risk-taking is important for success because it makes us aim for things that are difficult.

3. **Distracted** – We are programmed to be easily distracted by things we aren't concentrating on, particularly moving things. In evolutionary terms, being distractible is crucial for survival. If the hunter in ancient days focused so much on stalking a deer that he didn't notice the lion moving in the grass, that hunter was dead; if the gatherer was so focused on

picking berries and leaves that the snake slithering in the bushes went unnoticed, that gatherer was dead.

There's a fourth behaviour I want to mention. Although it's not connected to temptation and pleasure, it is important when we consider how life online can affect our mood and mental health. The fourth thing we are programmed to be is:

4. **Anxious** – When we hear a story of something bad happening, we naturally feel anxious; our heart rate rises and we are alert and jumpy. In evolutionary terms, this is also good for survival. If you heard about a lion killing someone in a nearby village, feeling anxious would make you be alert, ready to act. It would make you behave in a way that could save your life: you wouldn't want to go out alone or you'd take weapons with you; you'd be super-careful. That's what anxiety is for: to protect you.

So we are programmed to be social, curious, distracted and anxious. The Internet and social media give us opportunities to be all those things in bucketloads.

But when I say we are "programmed" or "wired" to be these things, what is happening in our brains? We need to understand this if we are to realize fully why we are so tempted to do the things we're programmed for.

In order to make us want to behave in a certain way, biology makes these behaviours feel rewarding or pleasurable. This is all about the reward system in the brain, the pathways and chemicals that are activated when we desire, seek and then experience pleasure. When we do what our biology wants us to do in order to survive, pleasure is the reward for doing it. It makes us do it more.

The proper name for the reward system is the mesolimbic pathway, a set of connected areas in the middle of your brain. It is one of a whole set of areas that tend to work in an instinctive "emotional" way rather than a controlled or "thinking" way. The mesolimbic pathway carries a hugely important chemical, a neurotransmitter called dopamine. Dopamine increases our desire for the thing that gives us pleasure.

I call dopamine the *yes* chemical, because it makes us want things and say *yes* to them. It is sometimes called the "pleasure chemical" and in many senses it is, but that slightly misses the important point: dopamine and the reward pathway are activated just *before* the rewarding act, when you *think* about the pleasurable act as well as when you *do* it. The fact that you feel this *before* means that you are *tempted* to do it. If you didn't feel the pleasure in advance, you might not be so tempted.

Take sugar as an example. Because sugar has lots of calories and we need calories to survive, we are wired to feel pleasure when we taste sweet things but also when we think about tasting sweet things, when we are looking forward to them. It's the same for all those other things we need: warmth, friendship, uplifting moods, discovering new things and physical contact. All these make us feel good, and thinking about them makes us want them.

That's all fine. We are wired to do things that give us pleasure because those things may help survival and success.

Trouble is, this brain wiring is from thousands of years ago, when food and shelter were scarce and there weren't so many people to be friends with. If sweet things hadn't given us pleasure all those thousands of years ago, we might not have spent valuable energy looking for them. If being warm didn't make us feel good, we might not have bothered to build strong, cosy shelters. If friendship didn't give us pleasure, we might not have dared to risk rejection or spend time building bonds and caring for each other.

It is this reward pathway that also plays a central role in all forms of addiction and bad habits. Getting pleasure from something doesn't always lead to us being addicted, of course: in fact, usually it doesn't. There are many other factors: genetic, environmental, psychological. But dopamine, the pleasure chemical, is crucial in addiction. The more (and more often) dopamine is activated in a person's reward circuits in the brain, the more likely that person is to go to great lengths (including dangerous risk-

taking) to get pleasure. Individuals with
levels or less active reward pathways
tempted: they are satisfied with less. The
might be less likely to have addictive behavio
are other factors that make some people m
vulnerable to addictive behaviours.

A famous set of experiments was carried out in t
1950s and 1960s. These experiments involved impl
a tiny transmitter in rats' brains so that every time
pressed a lever it stimulated their reward pathways –
other words, gave them a dopamine pleasure rush. In
one study, the rats chose to do this on average just over
29 times a minute – for twenty days! When they had the
choice of doing this or eating foods they liked, when
hungry, they still chose the brain stimulation option. This
was repeated in a similar study on humans in 1963.

However, though hundreds of studies have been
carried out in this area, it's important to realize that
stimulating one's brain with a lever is not the same as a
real-life pleasure, which is usually accompanied by a whole
load of thoughts and factors, and humans should be able
to control themselves better than rats. In fact, it was shown
that rats which had more stimulating environments were
less likely to press that pleasure lever. Still, the point is,
temptation is physical and powerful and that's important
to remember. And temptation and pleasure are connected
to the same processes that are activated during addiction

... already have worked

... rogrammed to be
... screens allow us
... ous (all that information
... ose "friends" out there), and
... distracting. When we are using
... are icons, adverts, links, some of them
... ying out for us to click on them to investigate
... y might lead to. Do you sometimes start looking
... something online and then find yourself going onto
other websites, being diverted from what you were first
looking for? And all those opportunities to connect with
other people, see their photos, share good or bad news,
ask for help, "like" each other's posts, accept a friendship,
react with emojis, see who has reacted to our posts –
these are social opportunities and we tend to grab them.
Think of those moments when you pick up your phone to
see if someone has messaged you – it's exciting, isn't it?
(And disappointing if there's nothing there.)

Second, you now know about the little rush of
dopamine, that burst of pleasure we feel when we do
things we are programmed to do. Remember that the
reward system is involved in temptation and addiction. If
we don't make an effort to moderate our behaviour, we

could become a bit like those rats, drawn towards pleasure over and over and over again. But remember that positive news – something people often miss when they talk about the rat experiments – that when rats were given a good environment, with lots of other exciting things to do, they didn't always go for the pleasure-inducing triggers; and for humans the same applies: when we are given other paths, other things to do, strong information and education, and an environment full of healthy opportunities, we also choose better options than simply going for pleasure over and over and over again. However, some people, for a variety of different reasons, really do become addicted and may neglect the other things they need in their lives. So we must all be aware of the temptations of online life, whether because we are genuinely at risk of addiction or simply because we want to avoid bad habits.

The other good and important news is that research suggests technology addiction is *different* from addiction to substances such as drugs and alcohol in two important ways. First, it's easier to control and cure because it doesn't damage our ability to manage our impulses, which addiction to drugs, for example, does. Second, it doesn't seem as though using our devices a lot makes us need them more, as happens with addictive substances. We just need to *want* to manage our social media and screen use and then learn how to.

What about the fact that we are programmed to be

anxious? That isn't connected to how tempting social media and screens are, but it's important when we realise how many opportunities and triggers for feeling anxious online life gives us. You'll read more about this in the sections **Social Life Online** and **The Internet and Mood**.

Summing Up

Social media and the screens we use to access the Internet are *very* tempting, largely because we are programmed to be curious, social and distracted, and when we are, we feel pleasure, which we want to repeat. Our devices can also feed our anxiety, which isn't pleasurable but is natural and biological.

This is why it is so easy for many of us to get into the habit of using our devices more than is healthy. If we don't understand that, we won't be aware of the dangers and we won't be strong enough to avoid them. Adults can get pretty judgemental about teenage use of smartphones, without realizing just how tempting and potentially addictive they can be. For them, too.

Understanding the power of our devices is good because then we can learn to control the hold they often have over us.

Are You Addicted to Your Smartphone or Tablet?

"Addiction" is a persistent compulsive use of something even when the user knows it is causing harm. "Persistent" means that it hasn't just been happening for a short time but has lasted a while. "Compulsive" means that you feel compelled to use or do the thing: you don't really want to stop, or else you're trying to stop, but you can't seem to manage.

Here's a simple test to see whether your smartphone use suggests you might be somewhat addicted. When I say "online", I mean anything you're doing on your phone or Internet-enabled device, whether on the Internet, on social media sites or while texting your friends. Try it if you dare!

A = Never or rarely
B = Sometimes
C = Often

1. How often do you stay online longer than you intended?
2. How often do you rush your homework because you spent too long online or want to go online?
3. How often do you check your messages before something else you need to do?
4. How often do you snap or act annoyed when someone bothers you while you are online?

5. How often do you try but fail to cut down the amount of time you spend online?
6. How often do you feel low, sad, tense or moody when you are not online, and this feeling goes away as soon as you are online?
7. How often do wish you could spend less time online because you feel guilty about your use?
8. How often does being online mean that you fall asleep too late?
9. How often do you try to hide or cover up how long you've been online or pretend that you're doing something useful when you're not?
10. How often have you been late or almost late or missed something because you were spending too long online?

How many Bs or Cs did you get? Score 1 for every B and 2 for every C. Because this isn't a scientifically valid test, I can't say which score definitely shows addictive tendencies, but I'd estimate that a total of 5 to 10 means you should take a look at your habits and use the strategies and knowledge in this book to take back more control. Any score over 10 may indicate that you have quite a strong set of bad habits that would benefit from action. And certainly any questions where you've given a C answer should alert you to some potentially unhealthy habits.

But don't worry: this book will empower you.

Oh, and now get your adults to take that test...

Another "if you dare" idea: look for one of the various free apps that monitors your smartphone usage. I won't mention any particular apps here, as more will have appeared by the time you read this. You know how to find them!

You'll find some tips and strategies to control and improve your screen use at the end of the book, under **Use Your New Powers**.

Being Safe Online

This book is about much more than safety: it's about living well and being healthy. You've probably had lots of messages about how to keep yourself safe, so you may feel you can skip this section. But online safety is really important, and survival skills need to come before enjoyment and usefulness. So, this section is essential but I'll keep it short.

HOW TO STAY SAFE

1. Don't give away information that can lead someone to know your real name or anything about where you live or go to school. Remember that information is also contained in photos: your school uniform, a street name, local landmarks. You may not think your privacy is important but the more information you make public, the easier it is for someone to trick or defraud

you. Be as private as possible, even if you think you don't care: you might change your mind later but once your information is out there, it's out there.

2. Learn to set strong passwords that can't be guessed. Never use a pet's name in a password. And be careful about security questions: often you are asked for your mother's maiden name; this is easy for someone to discover, so when you answer, make something up. (Just remember what you have chosen as your fake answer!) Set an especially strong password for your email because this will allow you to change any of the others. If someone else has your email address password, they can change everything, too... Change passwords every now and then.

3. Don't assume that people are telling the truth about themselves. They may not be and sometimes that can put you in great danger.

4. Never agree to meet someone you don't know in person. Even if you think you know them, perhaps because you've been communicating for a while, always go with someone else and meet in a public, busy place until you know you can trust them.

5. Be ultra-cautious of apps which allow you to live-stream video of yourself. They pose real dangers because they can make it very easy for a stranger to be watching you and then connect with you for sinister reasons. Never engage with someone you don't know

on these sites. Always remember you could be being watched by someone who wishes you harm.

6. If anything makes you uncomfortable, avoid it. Follow your instincts.

7. If you are worried about anything online, or if you think you've done something you now regret, talk to a trusted adult about it. Contact Childline if you don't want to tell someone who knows you.

8. If you're being bullied, hassled, victimized, trolled, threatened or insulted online, don't suffer alone. It's a truly horrible experience and any normal person would hate it and be really upset and affected. Talk to a trusted adult and don't suffer in silence. If it's happening to you in the privacy of your own room late at night, turn your device off, tell an adult immediately if possible, and do something quickly to take your mind off it. Try not to let it get to you: that's what the bullies want. How you feel now is not how you'll feel later, I promise: you can overcome and get over this.

9. Pornographic images or films online almost never represent normal, healthy sexual relationships. All relationships should be based on complete mutual consent; consent should never be forced (or it isn't consent); and no one should have to do anything they don't want. Watching porn can have a very unhealthy effect on someone's ability to be in good relationships, and it can also be addictive because it

powerfully triggers the pleasure systems in the brain.

10. Remember that possessing a photo of anyone under eighteen (including yourself) which has nudity or anything sexual about it is a criminal offence. So is sharing or sending such a photo. So is using such a photo as revenge. Any of these things can cause major problems for you so avoid at all costs. If you didn't realize this and believe you've done something you shouldn't have, talk to a trusted adult.

11. Keep informed. Make use of the excellent advice from organizations such as CEOP (Child Exploitation and Online Protection): its advice is based on huge experience and knowledge.

Summing Up

In short, stay in control of your information and your actions. That way, you can use and enjoy the Internet and have a good, healthy and safe life online. But if something goes wrong, it's not the end of the world, however bad it may feel right now. Get a trusted adult to help you work it out for the best.

Resources

You can look at Internet Live Stats yourself at **www. internetlivestats.com/internet-users/**

"The Zettabyte Era: Trends and Analysis" (updated in 2017) gives further Web statistics at **www.cisco.com/c/en/us/solutions/ collateral/service-provider/visual-networking-index-vni/vni- hyperconnectivity-wp.html**

Find more YouTube statistics by Statistic Brain at **www. statisticbrain.com/youtube-statistics/**

"How Many Websites Are There?" by Adrienne Lafrance in *The Atlantic*, Sept 2015 can be found at **www.theatlantic. com/technology/archive/2015/09/how-many-websites-are- there/408151/**

Read the MyGaming report, "There are 1.8 billion gamers in the world and PC gaming dominates the market" by Jamie McKane (2016), at **www.mygaming.co.za/news/ features/89913-there-are-1-8-billion-gamers-in-the-world-and- pc-gaming-dominates-the-market.html**

The 2015 Ofcom report, "The UK is now a smartphone society", is at **www.ofcom.org.uk/about-ofcom/latest/media/media- releases/2015/cmr-uk-2015**

"GenZ: The Limitless Generation – A Survey of the 13-18 Year-Old Wikia Audience" was conducted online by Ipsos MediaCT from the end of 2012 to February 2013. See **www.prnewswire. com/news-releases/generation-z-a-look-at-the-technology- and-media-habits-of-todays-teens-198958011.html**

"Generation Z: Meet the Young Millennials", a 2017 report about the music industry by BPI and ERA, also gives details of social media usage at **www.eraltd.org/news-events/press- releases/2017/generation-z-meet-the-young-millennials/**

The research involving rats and dopamine pathways was by James Olds and Peter Milner of McGill University in 1954. It is reported at **www.web.stanford.edu/group/neurostudents/cgi- bin/wordpress/?p=3733 and www.sciencedirect.com/topics/ neuroscience/brain-stimulation-reward**

The study repeated on humans in 1963 was by M. P. Bishop, S. T. Elder and R. G. Heath and is reported at **www.stanford.edu/ group/spanlab/Publications/bk06hsc_proof.pdf**

A study suggesting that addiction to smartphones is different from and may be easier to treat than substance addictions is "Brain Anatomy Alterations Associated with Social Networking Site (SNS) addiction" by Qinghua He, Ofir Tufel and Antoine Bechara (2017): **www.nature.com/articles/srep45064** (Note: it's a small study and the researchers point out that larger studies are needed.)

Walter Mischel's book, *The Marshmallow test: Understanding Self-Control and How to Master It* (2014), is fascinating on the subject of self-control.

The website of UK organisation CEOP (Child Exploitation and Protection) is **www.ceop.police.uk/safety-centre/**

ThinkUKnow is the education programme aimed at young people from the National Crime Agency's CEOP command: **www.thinkuknow.co.uk**

Childline is a free and confidential counselling service for any young person under nineteen: **www.childline.org.uk/ info-advice/bullying-abuse-safety/online-mobile-safety/ staying-safe-online/**

Internet Matters discusses online safety for teenagers at **www. internetmatters.org/advice/14plus/**

Ten tips on online safety from the BBC can be found at **www. bbc.co.uk/webwise/0/21259413**

Social Life Online

One of the most wonderful things about our smartphones and other screens is that they allow us many different opportunities to be social. And you now know that we are programmed to be social. It's in our nature. That doesn't mean we all love parties or chatting the whole time: many of us enjoy being peaceful and alone a lot, too; or prefer a deep conversation with one or two close friends, rather than a big group chat. What it means is that we have a natural need for friends and contacts who will help and support us. So we are powerfully drawn towards making social groups and bonds.

This is biological, physical, not just something society has created. It's not something we can – or should – get away from. We are not strong enough to do everything on our own: sometimes we're ill or sad or scared and then we need help; there may be a task we can't manage on our own; we might need to ask someone's advice; we may just prefer to do some things with other people, as a team working towards the same goal. In all those situations, and many more, we need someone to turn to. We need people we trust and are comfortable with. At first, we have the family unit we grew up in, our biological family or an adoptive family or some other unit of people who care for us. Often that family is a small household, with a wider family living elsewhere, connected by blood and legal relationships. Then, as we leave the security of that family unit, we make new groups at school, college, university, work and among the community we live in. New social networks.

Being excluded or not having good friends and networks is one of the most difficult things for us to deal with – in fact, it's bad for our well-being and mental health, and is a strong factor in mental illness such as depression. Our family and friends can help and protect us from both physical and mental harm.

This is why humans are so strongly wired to be social. Anything that allows us to do more of this social stuff is likely to be attractive to our brains and make us feel pleasure.

The phrase "social networks" has been around far longer than the Internet. But the Internet – and especially smartphones – has given us a whole load of new ways to build our social networks: different social media. Media is the plural of "medium", something that allows people to communicate, so the platforms we use for this – such as Instagram, Facebook, Snapchat, Twitter and more – are social media because they are used primarily by communities for communication. It's what they are designed for. And sites such as YouTube and Tumblr are, too, because even though one is a video and the other a blogging platform, they are also hugely social environments. You don't upload something to YouTube just for a way to pass the time: you do it hoping that people will see it and comment. You are making contact. Building connections.

Social networking is one of the main ways in which the Internet has quickly changed our lives, our choices and how we spend our time. These changes have affected many areas of our lives, for young people as well as adults of all ages, because social behaviour is important in our schools and workplaces as well as our homes and friendships.

Let's look at the positives and the negatives.

Positives

Some – adults, particularly – may not agree that all of these are positives. And, in fact, you'll find me mention some of them under negatives, too, although phrased differently. There are often two ways of looking at something and I want to suggest both ways. Let's look at the positives first.

MAKING AND KEEPING FRIENDS

Making friends can sometimes be difficult. Perhaps you live in a rural area where there aren't many people your age: social media gives you opportunities to keep in touch with your peers at school or friends you make on holiday. Perhaps you can't easily meet up with your school friends, because of transport difficulties, or because you are caring for a parent, or have responsibilities at home or a disability of your own. For you, the Internet and social media can really help in making friends and *keeping* contact with them – which is important for staying friends.

It's also great if you are naturally shy or quiet and find it difficult to know what to say at the start of a friendship. Using social media allows you to take your time and work out what you want to say and not feel self-conscious about people looking at you. For those who might describe themselves as socially awkward or anxious, this can be very reassuring and helpful. Lots of people don't like being in a large group, but when you're having a conversation online you can have the benefit of a group without feeling overwhelmed and under the spotlight. (There is a downside to this, too, which I'll talk about in the list of negatives.)

There's research that suggests not having any access to screen time and social media can have a negative effect. The Goldilocks hypothesis suggests that even if too much screen use might lead to problems, you can also have too little. This makes sense when you think about how social media can help you make friends and feel part of a group.

BROADER MINDS

When I was a teenager, the views I heard were those of my family and people at my school. Trust me when I say that that was a very narrow set of views! I had no chance to talk to people from other backgrounds, other cultures, other social classes. I had no idea what anyone thought outside my home and school; no idea what other people's lives were like.

OK, I might see things on television, but this wasn't a help, for two reasons. First, there were only three channels; and second, I couldn't talk to the people from these other lives. So I wasn't properly exposed to other people's opinions and world views. The only way round this was to have a "penfriend". Your penfriend would usually be from another country. Fantastic! Except ... you had to wait *weeks* for a letter to come back. Yes, I know: a letter. It was great getting those letters but most penfriend relationships fizzled out, as far as I could see.

Now you can easily chat online to people from other schools, regions, countries, cultures, backgrounds. You can read blog posts or comments or stories by ordinary people of every sort. And that's mind-opening. It makes you likely to be far more tolerant, more broad-minded and more empathetic than I was. When I look at my daughters and compare their open-mindedness and world knowledge with mine at their age, I'm amazed and even a bit ashamed.

EASY TO FIND PEOPLE JUST LIKE YOU

Just as social media makes it easy to have a wide range of friends with different lives and minds, it also makes it easy to find people just like you, with the same problems or in the same situations. And sometimes that's what you want and need. If you've got something going on in your life and there's no one in your school or amongst your existing friends who has that same issue, or for any reason you don't want to share it with them, there's likely to be somewhere online where people want to talk about that exact same thing. Or you might just want to chat about it to people you don't see every day.

There are a whole load of topics this might apply to, but I'm thinking of things like a difficult stepfamily situation; a medical condition or disability; questioning your gender identity or sexuality; an anxiety problem, such as social anxiety or a phobia; bereavement; someone you love being seriously ill; or any situation, whether temporary or permanent, where you feel you want to talk to someone who is going through the same, and you can't or don't want to talk to people you see or know "in real life".

The ability to connect with others who in some way are just like you helps you feel supported and not alone. There's no doubt many people find that their social media friends or followers can genuinely be a support network and help them through bad times and celebrate good times.

LEAVING A CONVERSATION

When you're with your friends and you've had enough of the conversation, or maybe you don't like how it's going, it's hard to leave without being obvious. Sometimes leaving a real conversation because you're annoyed or bored can look needy or draw attention to you for no good reason. But when you're chatting online, no one knows if you've left the room and gone to do something more interesting. You can even still be there, watching but not getting involved unless you want to.

HAVING SEVERAL CONVERSATIONS AT ONCE

In real life, you might be able to hear another group of people chatting about something way more interesting than the conversation you're stuck in. Online, you can do both! Yes, it can be hectic keeping up, but it can be good fun and exciting.

NOT HAVING TO WAIT FOR YOUR TURN TO SPEAK

There are lots of important rules of behaviour in face-to-face conversations: needing to wait till the right moment before you can speak, not interrupting someone who's speaking, taking turns, keeping the conversation going without silences. All those rules are irrelevant online. You can just say what you need to say when you want to say it. You're not interrupting, not being rude, but you're also not being dominated by louder, more confident people.

THINKING CAREFULLY ABOUT WHAT YOU WANT TO SAY

Often in face-to-face conversations, you have to say something quickly, before the moment passes. And sometimes it's difficult to get the wording right. Suppose someone has just told you about a worry and you're trying to think what's the most helpful or kind thing to say? Or someone has just said something that has really upset or angered you? In either of those situations, if you're online you can take as long as you need to work out the right thing to say. Of course, often people still *don't* say the right thing – and that's one of the big problems with online communication, as I'll talk about in a minute – but in theory, you have more opportunity to say something you won't regret.

Sometimes, you can even edit or delete your comment, depending on which platform or forum you're on. However, don't rely on this as there are plenty of ways in which the original can still be found. It's definitely not a good idea to have an argument and assume you can just delete or edit your words, but sometimes the possibility is there. My main point is that you have the *opportunity* of working out the wording you want before you commit it to the Web. But remember that even in a private forum, you are writing on that *World Wide* Web, where "private" is not a secure concept.

Some families find having a conversation online helps when they have to discuss things that are difficult or when face-to-face communication on a topic keeps descending into arguments or interruptions. Ideally, we should be able to have these discussions face to face but life isn't always ideal, is it? When people are angry or emotional, or when they are convinced that they are right, they often don't listen. And adults can more easily dominate as they may have the vocabulary and knowledge to sound more authoritative. So you could suggest at least starting a difficult discussion via one of the on-screen ways of communicating. Then *both* sides can take time to phrase their points clearly and read what the other side is saying. It takes the heat away.

These positives are enormous. I have made so many friends online, people I've often ended up meeting and being friends with offline, too. I can offer support to and receive support from a wide range of people I trust.

But there are also major disadvantages, some of them more likely than others. There are definitely things we all need to consider and watch out for. If I spend a lot more words writing about the negatives and possible negatives than the positives, it's not because I think that on balance this stuff is more bad than good. It's just that the negatives may not be so obvious but are, in my view, much more interesting. They are also more important for us all to think about because we may need to take steps to deal with them.

Negatives

Considering we are talking about "social" media, many aspects of behaviour online are pretty antisocial. You might even think some of the positives I listed are a bit antisocial: leaving a conversation, not having to wait for someone else to finish, being able to edit or delete your comments. But there are some more problematic negatives than that.

OVERUSE

You know the biology of why life online is so tempting and possibly addictive now. But why might it *matter* if you spend too long on social media? Here are some possible negatives which I think we need to consider.

1. You risk *not* spending time on other things that are important to health and well-being, such as physical exercise and face-to-face conversation.
2. You may not leave enough time for your school-work and you may end up rushing and not doing so well.
3. You may miss opportunities to stretch your mind or body in a variety of ways, such as with hobbies and new experiences.
4. You may become dependent on it and find it harder and harder to stop – and that's not a nice feeling because it means you are losing control.

HOW TO AVOID THIS NEGATIVE:

1. Use some of the strategies under **Tips for Good Screen Habits** at the end of the book.

2. Set yourself targets of the things you know you should do during the day and make sure you do those before spending time on social media. For example, if you know you've had plenty of exercise, eaten healthily and spent time talking or hanging out with friends or family, then it's not such a problem if you chill out on your favourite social media platform for an hour in the early evening.

(OVER)SHARING PERSONAL INFORMATION

Lots of people give themselves problems by oversharing personal information online. Often this ends up being just minor embarrassment, but sometimes it can be worse than that. The thing is, online is just so public. You think you're just showing a photo or telling something to one close friend or a small group of friends but, before you can say "delete", it's spread and could soon be seen by huge numbers of total strangers.

If we know this, why do we do it? Why do people, young and old, keep falling into the trap of saying or showing too much, revealing things about themselves that they wouldn't shout out to a room full of strangers?

Again, it's that socially wired brain. Scientists have discovered that every time we share personal information with another human being, we get a little rush of that reward chemical, dopamine. Remember how those rats kept on triggering their brains' reward systems instead of eating or drinking? We love the feeling, so it's easy to keep on doing it.

I should point out that lots of people manage to resist doing this. I know people of all ages who are incredibly careful and extremely private online. I'm very careful myself. But even when we *are* careful, we are often gradually building up an online story of ourselves in more detail than we may realize, and if we ever want to change or remove that story it is virtually impossible.

You may have heard that employers sometimes check a candidate's online and social media presence before hiring them. And there are pieces of software that claim to be able to work out your personality, religion, opinions and political views just from what you've said or liked or shared on social media. To protect against this, many countries are at various stages of agreeing a legal "right to be forgotten", which allows people in some circumstances to have things about their past removed from Internet searches. After all, it isn't fair that something you did or views you expressed when you were a young teenager should follow you your whole life, especially if they weren't illegal. So, removing your Internet history may soon be possible, but it's best not to rely on it. Much better just to be as careful as possible now.

HOW TO AVOID THIS NEGATIVE:

1. Don't post anything till you've had time to think about it. Train yourself into the mindset that posting online is like crossing a road: you wouldn't do it without stopping and looking both ways.
2. Keep reminding yourself that people can easily get wrong impressions of you, and try to think of that while you post.
3. Don't post anything you wouldn't mind being seen by your grandma or any other person. And consider nothing to be completely private: even if you're in a private conversation, it could go public.

ONLINE DISINHIBITION EFFECT

This connects directly to oversharing. The online disinhibition effect describes how our communications are usually less careful and less inhibited when we aren't actually with the other person. John Suler, the psychologist who made this theory well known, divided this into "benign" and "toxic" disinhibition, because sometimes it leads to good results, such as being more willing to help people, and sometimes to bad results, involving sexting (sending images or words of a sexual nature), verbal abuse, trolling and bullying.

Suler says there are several reasons why this happens. We are anonymous and invisible, for example. Often the behaviour doesn't happen in real time so it doesn't feel as though it's "now". We easily misinterpret someone's tone because we aren't actually hearing their voice or seeing their face, so we can think someone is being hostile when they're not, which makes us more angry.

Once we realize that it's likely we and others may fall into these traps, we can have more control. We can say to ourselves, "Hang on: this isn't the best way to have a discussion because we are all affected by not being able to see each other. That person was rude because they can't see me. How about I just walk away and stop worrying about it?"

We can be more rational and controlled once we understand the problem. You'll often see Twitter arguments come to an end when one person says, "Yeah, a tweet's not the best way to discuss complicated problems!"

HOW TO AVOID THIS NEGATIVE:

1. Remember that people are more likely to be mean online. It doesn't excuse them but it may explain some negative behaviour.
2. Try to rein in your own impulses. Think about the moral high ground: in other words, how good it can feel to be the person who behaves better than others, rather than worrying that you might have crossed a line.
3. If you have been angrier or ruder than you intended, read your messages back to yourself the next day and

if they make you cringe and wish you hadn't sent them, remember that feeling and use it to help you not do it the next time. Three deep breaths and walk away!

4. If things are getting out of hand with people behaving badly, talk to an adult you trust.

LACK OF PRIVACY

Balanced against our drive to be social is our need for privacy. Some people don't seem to mind very much about this but others do. I imagine everyone has some things they want to be private, though. In the online world, the only way to have the privacy we want is by being very, very careful. And, of course, sometimes we still slip up or someone might invade our privacy and share stuff against our will. Parents can often be guilty of this, and the word "sharenting" describes the annoying (and often undermining) habit some parents have of posting online their children's embarrassing moments. I believe it's unfair and wrong to share online images or stories about people you love without their consent – and often the children are too young really to have control of that consent.

Do we have a *right* to privacy? Yes and no. There are certain rights that the law gives us (and these will be different in different countries). For example, no one is allowed to come into your house without permission or set up a CCTV camera looking into your bedroom. But there are many ways in which you might think you're being private – having a private conversation, for example, but someone else might hear it, whether accidentally or because the person you were talking to shared it. It's always been true that a secret can spread, of course, but there are two things about social media that take this several steps further: first, it's so easy to screenshot or share your post or image; second, once that's happened, it's incredibly easy for it to spread fast and wide. And once it's out there, it's almost impossible to get back. (The next point about sexting and posting images makes this very relevant.)

There are different degrees of privacy, though. There are things you'd be happy for your close friends to know but not your family, and there may be things you're happy for your family to know but not your friends, or at least not all friends. And then there's what you don't want your school or the whole world to know.

Let's not exaggerate the problems: most things that you don't want to be public will never be public, mainly because most things about most ordinary people are not that interesting. So, even if a "secret" gets out, it's most likely to be a very minor embarrassment and quickly forgotten by those who found out.

However, it's also true to say that most people's lives are not as private as they used to be, and sometimes not as private as many of us would like. Privacy – even though we each need it differently – is something that makes us feel secure. Getting the amount of privacy you need is important to your well-being, and that can be threatened by social media.

HOW TO AVOID THIS NEGATIVE:

1. Think about how important privacy is to you and which aspects of your life you'd most like to keep private. Think about how you will do your best to achieve that.
2. Check all privacy settings on apps and devices you use.
3. Don't feel you have to do anything that you don't want to do. Don't be on social media if you're not comfortable: lots of people stay away or use it very carefully.
4. Ask your parents or carers not to post images or stories about you without your permission, even if they think it's in a family group on Facebook, for example. Would they like it if you posted pictures and embarrassing stories about them?

SEXTING AND POSTING IMAGES

There is one way the law does protect your privacy, and it's extremely important to know this. The details will differ in different countries, but in the UK, the law is clear: posting, sharing, sending, threatening to send or even possessing an image that could be considered "rude", intimate or sexual of anyone under eighteen is illegal. Even if the photo is of the person sending it. So, a naked photo, a photo of genitalia, an "underwear shot", a topless photo of a girl, a photo with a sexual message – all these are potentially breaking the law. Make sure your friends understand this law, as it's so easy to be on the wrong side of it.

The online disinhibition effect explains that people often don't use their best judgement when online. And my point about how we get pleasure from revealing personal information is also relevant. Both these things help understand why people sometimes share too much.

Many countries are becoming stricter about this in an effort to protect teenagers and children from the nightmare possibilities when an "indecent" or embarrassing photo is shared. "Shared" means sent to one person, two people, or the world. It doesn't matter. One reason for strict laws is that these photos can often end up on paedophile sites.

Revenge porn is also illegal in the UK, whatever your age. This is where someone, usually after a relationship break-up, takes revenge by sending sexual photos of their former partner to other people.

Often young people at the start of a relationship feel they have to send sexy pictures of themselves, and one half of the couple might try to persuade the other to do that. "If you like me, you'd do it." "You're so uptight." "It's just a photo – what's the harm?" I can understand why it's easy to feel pressured, especially if the pressure keeps going on and on, but you'll feel so much better if you resist.

HOW TO AVOID THIS NEGATIVE:

1. Ask yourself what would happen if you said no. Would your boy/girlfriend drop you? Really? If so, do you want to stay with someone who would do that?

2. You might be tempted to do what you're being asked, but stop and think. How would you feel about strangers seeing this photo? Once you've clicked "send", you've lost control of it. Your "friend" might not be your friend for ever, and accidents happen – what if someone else gets hold of their phone?

3. Think of ways to reply to the pressure to send a naked photo or sext: "If you liked me, you wouldn't ask me." "I'm not stupid." "I'm better than a photo." "No. Not happening." "Take a shower."

4. If someone sends you anything you think comes into this category, delete it immediately. If you can, ask the person to stop. If they don't, ask a trusted adult.

5. If you're in a group that shares a photo of this sort, delete it from your phone. If possible, explain why sharing a photo like this is an illegal, wrong and dangerous thing to do. If you can't do that, talk to a trusted adult.

6. CEOP, the Child Exploitation and Online Protection organization, gives great advice about what to do if you are worried about any behaviour online, and also what to do if you have already shared a photo or had one shared by someone else.

A very important note:

If this has happened to you already, please don't panic, even if the law has been broken. Take a deep breath and see a trusted adult as soon as possible so they can start to sort the problem. People make mistakes and young people should be forgiven. Whatever has happened, it's not the end of the world and you will be able to put it behind you. But you need help to sort it first. How you feel about it now is not how you will feel about it in the future, trust me.

EVERYONE'S PERFECT LIVES

Everyone seems to have perfect lives on social media. They post pictures of their amazing weekend/party/holiday/boyfriend/girlfriend. On Instagram or wherever, there are all those beautiful faces with perfect smiles. There's even a particular "selfie smile", according to historian Professor Colin Jones, who has written about the history of the smile. There's special make-up for photos, as I discovered when a sales assistant asked if I wanted "photo-finish" make-up.

And I noticed during Christmas 2017 that it seemed to be almost compulsory to put your perfect family Christmas photo on Facebook. When I saw these posed, glossy, cosy photos of smiling families with champagne glasses raised to the camera and tables groaning with gorgeous food, it made me wonder what seeing them must feel like for people whose Christmas was very different: perhaps sad or lonely or without the money to afford the party glitz. And I bet some of those perfect photos disguised arguments and stress.

It's easy to start thinking that everything and everyone just looks so much more gorgeous or rich or popular or exciting than you and your life. You see that stunning photo of someone and then you look in the mirror when you've just woken up and you think you don't compare. It's hard not to measure ourselves against others and very easy to be dissatisfied with our lives, faces, bodies, personalities. Donna Freitas, in her book *The Happiness Effect*, draws on her own research into self-esteem of young adults in the US. There's evidence elsewhere (though this is hard to measure accurately and the studies that suggest this are usually small-scale or very specific) that young people who spend a lot of time online tend to be more anxious and have lower self-esteem than those who are more moderate in their use, and it's hard not to feel that constantly comparing oneself with others' super-positive social media posts could be at least partly to blame. I'll mention this again in the section **The Internet and Mood**.

HOW TO AVOID THIS NEGATIVE

1. Keep reminding yourself of the truth: people are putting their best bits out there; those selfies are probably the result of a hundred and fifty attempts and a few YouTube videos describing how to get the lighting right.

2. Watch one of the Dove Campaign for Real Beauty videos that show how make-up and image-changing software is used to create the so-called "perfect" images you see in adverts.

3. Try to spend time (online and offline) with friends who don't make you feel bad like this.

4. Do your best to focus on the more important things in life. It's hard to ignore feelings of low self-esteem but easier if you can find more positive and inspiring activities. A hobby, challenge, real-life stories of inspiration, something to be involved in mentally or physically – these will help you not to dwell on undermining thoughts.

LIKE-SPAMMING: COMPETITION FOR "LIKES"

People tend to want "likes", whatever social media platform they're on. (Sometimes they aren't called "likes" but "favourites" or anything else that a reader clicks to indicate approval.) So, when we post something, we're hoping people will "like" it, otherwise we may worry that what we said was boring or that no one likes us.

I confess that if I posted something on Facebook and *no one* clicked the little "like" button, I'd be a bit disappointed. I'd wonder why. If no one had liked it after a while, I might even quietly take it down and go away and do something else. Then I'd soon forget about it. It wouldn't rock my self-esteem.

But then my self-esteem is not too bad. And usually someone does like my posts, because I only hang out with people I really know. I'd be quite happy with just a few likes – I don't need hundreds. Or even dozens.

But ... what if I *regularly* got no likes? What if all my friends were getting gazillions and I was consistently failing to? What if my self-esteem were really low and I was struggling to work out who I was and whether I was worth anything? What if I kept trying and still kept failing? What if I really did think everyone was more interesting and popular than me? It could start to dominate my life and erode my fragile confidence.

This is where the temptation to like-spam can come in. Social media is full of unspoken rules, and one of them is that if someone responds to your post you should usually respond to theirs. So, if you go and like everyone's posts or comments or pictures, they might do the same for you. That's the start of like-spamming, and on its own it's maybe not such a big deal. Until you find that there are pieces of software that will do it for you, liking everything your friends post.

You might still argue it's not harming anyone, but it feels wrong to trick a friend into thinking you like what they said just so that they will like what you said.

It certainly deserves its place on the list of negatives.

HOW TO AVOID THIS NEGATIVE

1. Keep it real. If you really like something, say so – that's proper friendship and support. It will also make you feel good because you're giving a bit of praise to someone else. It's a valid way to build a friendship. And if you've done it genuinely and voluntarily and the other person does the same back, excellent!

2. Ask yourself if it really makes sense to measure your self-worth according to whether people who hardly know you can be bothered to respond to something you said. Tell yourself that you are worth more than this.

TROLLING AND CYBERBULLYING

The online disinhibition effect can sometimes lead to these two nasty behaviours. They are similar to each other but not identical. In some ways, trolling is just plain silly, whereas cyberbullying is often much nastier and can be horribly undermining to self-esteem. But what exactly is the difference?

Trolling is when, often for no obvious reason, someone gets pleasure from goading a person online, usually anonymously. The troll is trying to annoy the other person so much that they react, but the troll doesn't really care about the results. Trolling ranges from name-calling and insults to disgusting threats of violence. It is designed to intimidate and harass and is usually directed at someone the troll has never met. Often a troll begins by posting a random spiteful comment or deliberate disagreement in a comment thread or on any social media platform, and then keeps on at it, with the intention to annoy and provoke reaction.

Anyone can be unlucky enough to be trolled. It is usually best ignored because the troll only does it for a reaction. There's a phrase: "Don't feed the troll." They can be slippery creatures and if you try to engage with them they often say something completely irrelevant. It's important not to underestimate them, though, as the damage and fear they can cause their victims is huge. I have some advice below, if you should be so unlucky as to fall victim to one of these nasty people.

There are certain communities and certain behaviours where trolling is more likely. The more successful you are, the stronger and more vocal your opinions, the more you engage online in large forums, and the more you engage in the adult world, the more likely this is to happen. There are some seriously nasty people out there who do not want you to have a voice and they get very angry when you do.

How is cyberbullying different? Well, often they are

the same or similar, but the underlying difference is that, whereas a troll doesn't really care how the victim feels, a cyberbully does: cyberbullying aims to frighten, control or hurt the victim. Cyberbullying tends to be nastier and more personally directed (and when trolls continue to focus on an individual, that's when it becomes no different from cyberbullying). Also, cyberbullying often involves several people doing the bullying at once, whereas trolls tend to work alone, though they often target whole forums, posting outrageous or plain silly comments and interfering with everyone else's desire to work well together. Bullies get their strength from thinking they are stronger than the victim; trolls get their strength from simply being anonymous and annoying and seeking attention.

Trolls are disruptive, annoying, spiteful. Bullies are cruel, controlling, aggressive. And trolls can become bullies and bullies will enjoy trolling. They all deserve our disrespect.

HOW TO AVOID THIS NEGATIVE:

1. If someone has decided to troll or bully you, there's almost certainly nothing you could have done to prevent it. Always remember that the trolls or bullies are at fault. This is about them, not you.
2. Stick to forums where this behaviour isn't tolerated and where discussion is respectful. If you're part of a

friendship group which often has this problem, talk to your good friends about how to prevent it.

3. If someone makes a spiteful remark, whether you think this is trolling, bullying or whatever, the best response at first is usually to ignore it. It can be quite mild and may even disappear. But do take a screenshot, just in case this situation worsens, so that you have evidence if necessary.

4. If this becomes at all persistent, or if anything makes you feel worried or uncomfortable, talk to a trusted adult. If it's happening at school or outside but amongst people from your school, the school should deal with it. Of course, reporting a bully is a tricky thing to do, but it's really important that you don't have to deal with this alone. Keep evidence of everything and a diary of when each incident happens.

5. If anyone ever, even once, threatens you with sexual or other physical violence, tell a trusted adult. It doesn't matter whether they mean it or not: it's not acceptable and may be illegal.

6. If anyone ever threatens to send or share a photo of you that is in any way sexual, naked or "rude", remember it's against the law. If you feel safe to do so, calmly remind the person of this. If not, tell an adult before the person goes ahead with their threat.

TOO MANY FRIENDS

Yes, you can have too many friends! If you or your adults are interested in the science behind this, look at the work of evolutionary psychologist Robin Dunbar. Friendships and social groups require "maintenance" because you have to build bonds and maintain them enough to keep them going. If you meet someone one day, enjoy being with them, but then never communicate or engage in any way, that is very unlikely to become a friendship. Of course, there are different levels of friendship and closeness, from best friends and family groups to friends that you know fairly well and then people who are just acquaintances.

The point is, if a connection is to be useful and strong, it needs actions by both parties to build bonds. Dunbar's work, based on comparing behaviours and brain sizes of several mammals, including humans, suggests that the maximum number of "friends" that each human can manage is 150. More than that, and some of them will have to drift away. There just aren't enough hours in the day to do the things necessary to keep more connections going.

Many – probably most – people who engage with social media will have more than 150 "friends" and sometimes many hundreds of them. But we can't really *know* that many people. When a real friend is going through a bad time, we want to help them; when they are going through a good time, we want to share that pleasure. We want to give them a hug – whether online or in real life – and say something to show we care. But we can't do that for too many people. Of course, we might say we care about millions of people we've never met but we wouldn't say that those people are our friends if we've never had any contact at all.

Having too many friends – whether you believe that number is 150 or something bigger or smaller – can be stressful because you can't succeed in managing all those friendships. You can't do the necessary virtual hugging and sympathy.

I suggest that the effort of trying is exhausting, as well as stressful because you may feel inadequate. I know I do, when I go on Facebook and find several friends saying something about either a really good or a really bad thing that's happened. I feel I should respond to everyone – they are my *friends* after all. But I often can't.

With so many connections that you don't really know, you may think they all care about you, when some of them can't. So you may trust them when you shouldn't.

HOW TO AVOID THIS NEGATIVE:

1. Understand that many people you are connected to online may be good people, but if you don't know much about them you can't really count them as friends.

2. Have as much control as you can over who you are

online friends with. Try to make sure you do know something about them.

3. If you limit the amount of time you spend on social media, you will find that your friendship group remains manageable anyway.

4. Try not to measure your value – or the value of anyone else – according to how many online friends you have. Having lots of online friends just says you're on your phone or computer a lot, which is really not a way to measure your value.

NOT PRACTISING ESSENTIAL COMMUNICATION SKILLS

I believe that online communication skills and face-to-face (or speaking on the phone) communication skills are both important. They can be useful in different circumstances. Either of them can be quicker, more effective, more fun, or better at getting a point over, depending on the situation. They both have to be practised so that we learn all the little rules of communication and how to make sure that, wherever possible, we say exactly what we mean and the other person gets exactly what we meant.

I also think that very often, face-to-face or phone communication is more difficult than online or via text. And it's natural to want to avoid difficult things. But if we avoid a difficult thing too often, we won't learn the skills.

Why might it be more difficult?

1. Most people can be a bit shy sometimes. Making eye contact with a stranger or someone you don't know well can be challenging.
2. You don't have time to think of the exact words. Some people find their words come together easily; others not so much. I find that topics I talk about a lot I'm very fluent in whereas others I can be more hesitant about: proof that practising talking makes it easier.
3. A dominant and confident person can take over a conversation, leaving you unable to express yourself.

But, especially if we're one of those who find talking most difficult, we need to learn to use and practise using our voice because it is a powerful tool, allowing us to make friends and connections, persuade people of our views, feel comfortable around others, be confident and entertain or inspire others. It can help us in our relationships and working opportunities, and improve our chances to express ourselves.

So don't allow your voice to become small and weak from disuse. It's an instrument: keep practising it.

HOW TO AVOID THIS NEGATIVE:

1. Take small opportunities to speak out loud to people, either face to face or on the phone. Casual conversations are all you need: asking someone the time, asking whether this is the right bus, ordering

a coffee or checking the ingredients of a food item, buying tickets.

2. If you're nervous, take a big breath before speaking, so that your voice comes out nice and strong.

3. Don't expect to find it easy to talk to strangers at first. Most people – and certainly most young people – find it really hard. You just have to keep doing it and it gets easier.

A very important note:

Some people have a condition called social anxiety (sometimes called social phobia), which means that interacting with or speaking to people is harder for them than it is for others, causing extreme anxiety and even panic. Sometimes it can be impossible to speak.

There's also a condition called selective mutism where people are unable to speak in certain situations. It's as though something is blocking the words from coming out. The word "selective" is a bit misleading, as sufferers are not making a choice not to speak.

If these things apply to you, or you think they might, see a doctor, who can direct you towards the right help.

IGNORING FRIENDS AND FAMILY

How do you feel when you are with someone and they are on their phone instead of properly being with you? Or you're trying to tell your friend a story but she keeps glancing at her phone or texting while "listening"? Or you want to tell your mum or dad something but they're "busy" on their phone or a phone call just has to be taken first?

Welcome to the world of phubbing: snubbing someone by being on a phone.

Different people have different levels of tolerance for this, but I don't believe it's particularly age-related. I have friends my own age who will have their phone on the table while we're having lunch together, and I've been left at the dinner table when the person I'm with goes to take a call which I know isn't an emergency. I know adults who have major arguments about whether it's OK to watch TV together while one person is on social media. I've been bumped into on pavements by more phone-fixated adults than young people. And when I ask teenagers in schools whether their parents are ever on the phone when the teenagers want to talk, a forest of hands goes up!

What kind of message does this send? "You're not as important or interesting as this message from another friend." "Yes, I'm listening to you – just not 100%, but that's OK because I don't need 100% for you." "Watching TV or having a meal with you is fun but it would be a whole lot more fun if Jack/Jill were here, too."

It's worth pointing out that in "the old days" many adults (mostly men, I'd say) did something just as antisocial: read the newspaper at the breakfast table. They probably used the same excuse: "This is important. More important than you: you'll wait." But really they were being selfish, antisocial and avoiding conversation. At least the paper only came once a day. Our phones feed us endlessly if we let them.

Some young people have come up with a new piece of etiquette called "the rule of three". This says that if there are at least three people in your group who are talking, it's OK to sneak a look at your phone. Sherry Turkle is a researcher who has investigated and written about how human interaction can be changed by smartphone and device use, concluding that the conversation that happens while people in a group are dipping in and out of their phones is shallow, fractured and avoids "big topics". She writes: "In a 2015 study by the Pew Research Center, 89 percent of cellphone owners said they had used their phones during the last social gathering they attended. But they weren't happy about it; 82 percent of adults felt that the way they used their phones in social settings hurt the conversation."

A fascinating study in 2012 offers another reason for not having your phone out while talking to a friend. In it, strangers were asked to chat for ten minutes. Half had their mobile phones on the table during their conversation, while the others had a notebook instead. Those who had their phones in sight reported that they were less likely to be friends with the other person and felt less close to them.

It seems it may really be true that our phones can come between us in some way. The researchers didn't test whether the same would be true of a landline phone – personally, I think if any phone was sitting there on a dining table it could be off-putting, but they usually aren't there; they're usually in another room.

HOW TO AVOID THIS NEGATIVE:

1. It's very simple: put your phone away! (On silent, not vibrate.)

2. There are very few world-shattering situations that can't wait till you've finished your meal, coffee, programme, meeting. And if you genuinely are in such a situation, explain. Tell the truth.

3. Insist on a tech-free family dinner for everyone who's in the house at the time. If this rule came from you, the teenagers, this would be fantastic. It gives you all a chance to say what's happened during your day. If this is very difficult – and in some situations it might be – you could have the news on the radio. That would avoid painful silences and give you something to talk about. But there's nothing wrong with silence – don't be afraid of it.

4. Make sure that any rules in your household or group are for everyone. That's adults, too.

Summing Up

Remember: I'm not saying social media is overall a bad thing. I'm not saying whether it's more bad than good (even though I seem to have come up with a lot of negatives!), because I don't think I can answer that. There are huge positives, and all the negatives can be avoided, once we know what they might be.

I hope you've had no unpleasant experiences on social media and that you never do. Maybe you already are brilliantly in control and have just the right number and quality of online friendships. If so, well done and lucky you! If you have already had some trouble or if you just feel for any reason you're spending too much time on social media, I hope you realize you're very much not alone in that. It's very tempting and can be so pleasurable, for reasons you now know.

For your own health and well-being, though, keep it under control – your control. Don't look at what other people are doing: do what is right for you, and you alone. And if you need help, ask for it.

Resources

"A Large-Scale Test of the Goldilocks Hypothesis Quantifying the Relations Between Digital-Screen Use and the Mental Well-Being of Adolescents" by Andrew K. Przybylski and Netta Weinstein is reported by myScience at **www.myscience.org/ news/2017/moderate_amounts_of_screen_time_may_not_be_ bad_for_teenagers_well_being-2017-oxford** and in more detail by Big Think at **www.bigthink.com/david-ryan-polgar/is-screen-time-bad-for-kids-researchers-find-the-positive-sweet-spot**

Scientists found that we get a rush of dopamine when we post information about ourselves. See "Disclosing information about oneself is intrinsically rewarding" by Diana I. Tamir and Jason P. Mitchell (2012) at **www.pnas.org/content/109/21/8038.abstract**

You can find more information about John Suler's "online disinhibition effect" at **www.learning-theories.com/online-disinhibition-effect-suler.html**

The website of UK organization CEOP (Child Exploitation and Protection) is **www.ceop.police.uk/safety-centre/**

To read more about sexting, visit the Family Lives website at **www.familylives.org.uk/advice/teenagers/online/sexting/**

Colin Jones has written about the history of the smile, as discussed in Rozina Sabur's 2017 article, "Selfies have ruined the smile, historian claims", at **www.telegraph.co.uk/**

news/2017/06/02/selfies-have-ruined-smile-historian-claims/

"Media Use, Face-to-Face Communication, Media Multitasking and Social Well-Being Among 8-12-Year-Old Girls" by Roy Pea, Clifford Nass, Lyn Meheula et al (2012) suggests girls of that age who use social media more tend to be more anxious. The study is available at **www.researchgate.net/publication/221769567_Media_Use_Face-to-Face_Communication_Media_Multitasking_and_Social_Well-Being_Among_8-_to_12-Year-Old_Girls** and is widely reported elsewhere.

Although people have argued that what you do online is more important than how much time you spend, a study by Holly B. Shakya and Nicholas A. Christakis (2017) – "A New, More Rigorous Study Confirms: The More You Use Facebook The Worse You Feel" – contradicts this, citing quantity as being more important than quality. They talk about their research at **www.hbr.org/2017/04/a-new-more-rigorous-study-confirms-the-more-you-use-facebook-the-worse-you-feel**

Donna Freitas's book, *The Happiness Effect: How Social Media Is Driving a Generation to Appear Perfect at Any Cost* (2017), draws on her interviews with young people.

Find some of the Dove Campaign for Real Beauty videos at **www.dove.com/uk/stories/campaigns.html**

You can hear Robin Dunbar's 2017 talk, "Is There a Limit to How Many Friends We Can Have?", at **www.npr.org/2017/01/13/509358157/is-there-a-limit-to-how-many-friends-we-can-have**

For more on social anxiety, visit Social Anxiety UK's website at **www.social-anxiety.org.uk**

Demos conducted a study into abuse on Twitter in 2017 – "Male celebrities receive more abuse on Twitter than women" – which you can read about at **www.demos.co.uk/press-release/demos-male-celebrities-receive-more-abuse-on-twitter-than-women-2/**

Sherry Turkle, professor at Massachusetts Institute of Technology, has studied how smartphones have altered conversation. She is the author of *Alone Together: Why We Expect More From Technology and Less From Each Other* (2011) and, more recently, *Reclaiming Conversation: The Power of Talk in a Digital Age* (2015). Her article "Stop Googling. Let's Talk" (2015) is at **www.nytimes.com/2015/09/27/opinion/sunday/stop-googling-lets-talk.html**

Pew Research Center produced a 2015 study entitled, "Americans' Views on Mobile Etiquette", which you can read at **www.pewinternet.org/files/2015/08/2015-08-26_mobile-etiquette_FINAL.pdf**

"How the mere presence of a mobile phone harms face-to-face conversations" examines Andrew K. Przbylski and Netta Weinstein's 2012 study into this issue: **www.digest.bps.org.uk/2012/09/24/how-the-mere-presence-of-a-mobile-phone-harms-face-to-face-conversations/**

The Knowledge and Information Explosion

The amount of information on the Web is massive and the Internet allows us access to pretty much any fact about anything that has ever been recorded. We've always been hungry for knowledge. When I was a teenager, people used to come to the door selling encyclopedias; they were incredibly expensive but families would buy them – whole sets of them – even though they were going to go out of date fairly soon.

Gone are the days when we had to rely on encyclopedias, textbooks or experts who had spent years learning about their special topic (although those experts are still very worth relying on). Now, anyone who wants to know about something, whether general knowledge or something really specialized, just has to open their phone or computer and within a few taps of the keyboard the information is there.

We don't really know how much "information" is on the Internet. You'll see figures but they tend to include texts, Facebook posts, tweets, and such like, most of which isn't information in the sense that it would inform you or increase your knowledge. I've mentioned a figure already, under **How Big Is It?**, when I quoted Daniel Levitin as saying that we've created 3,000 exabytes of data, but this will have grown considerably since those figures were collected. He also refers to research that suggests that in 2011 Americans took in five times as much information as in 1986 – the equivalent of 175 newspapers; that during our leisure time we process 100,000 words; and that TV stations produce 85,000 hours of new programming a day. The website Internet Live Stats, as seen in March 2018, says, "Google now processes over 40,000 search queries every second on average." And, according to Statista, "As of July 2015, more than 400 hours of video content were uploaded to YouTube every minute. You'll find other mind-boggling statistics to illustrate just how much is "out there."

So, what are the positives and negatives of what is obviously an enormous – and growing – amount of information and potential "knowledge"? And what does it mean when we say we "take in" this much information?

Positives

EASY AND QUICK TO FIND FACTS AND ANSWERS

Not only is the information out there: it's usually very easy to find. Once you've learnt a few basic methods of putting phrases into your chosen search engine, it has now become so efficient that you are most likely to find what you're looking for in the first few results. And you have a chance to compare the results, too, if you're not sure whether the first answer you get is correct.

It's not just easy; it's also quick. Before the Internet, if you needed to find something out, you *might* have had the relevant books in the house but you probably didn't. Most likely you'd have had to wait till you could go to a library; for many people that wasn't just round the corner; or it might not have been open; and even then, the right books might not have been there and you'd have had to order them. Now most people can get online within seconds or minutes.

This has made life easier in many ways for so many people: writers like me, teachers looking for good quality information to direct their students to, individuals just wanting to know something, and students like you, investigating something for school.

BECOMING GOOD AT SKIM-READING

It seems likely that we may be becoming better at grabbing the key facts out of an article and reading things quickly. After all, that's what we spend a lot of time doing, and we tend to improve at what we spend a lot of time doing. As long as the key facts are sufficient for what we want, that's a benefit.

Website designers and online writers may even

make use of the knowledge that, when people read for information, most read in a certain pattern, moving their eyes in an F-shape across the page: headline first, skim down the left-hand side, and then go back to about a third of the way down the page. Writers can then put the keywords and facts in those areas and be reasonably sure that the readers will pick them up. (This, of course, can also lead to a negative result, as I'll mention below.)

Being able to read something quickly and get the key information out of it is a useful skill, especially in this busy age.

ANYONE CAN BECOME AN EXPERT

There was a time when being an expert was a privilege that only a few could have. You'd usually have to become an academic attached to a university, spending years doing original research before you could be regarded as knowing a great deal about a subject and have people ask your advice. It was difficult to be self-taught because the top-rate information wouldn't have been accessible to you until you read the books written by the experts. And just reading a book or three doesn't make you an expert.

Now it's possible for people to read, study and understand the original research, which is generally all available online. You have to pay for some of it but most of it is free. It's also possible to make contact with the academics who have done the research and to engage in the arguments that always arise around any topic, enabling you to really understand it.

So, expertise has become democratized. It's not a guarded secret any more. You don't have to join a special club of experts.

But not everyone has equal access. We tend to assume that everyone can easily access information but there are people who are excluded, through poverty, weak reading skills, disabilities or even poor broadband connections.

EASY TO SHARE YOUR OWN KNOWLEDGE

Once you know enough about something, you can write about it yourself and share that knowledge. Young people have done this really successfully. Zoella became world-famous (and rich) from her vlogging on beauty and well-being for teenagers. Charlie McDonnell, musician and film-maker, had the first UK YouTube channel to reach a million viewers. The Mile Long Bookshelf and Physics Girl are both successful well-known blogs started by young women.

But you don't have to aim to be famous. If you know about something, you can write about it via the Internet. You can start your own blog or even write and self-publish a book.

Many authors of books, both fiction and non-fiction, have websites or blogs that showcase their own expertise on a topic and also have links to research and resources.

Sharing this knowledge is free and requires very few technical skills, which are all easy to learn.

AMAZING APPS AND TOOLS

With apps that are often free or almost free, we can very quickly discover many more types of information than simple factual knowledge: where we are, if we're lost; how to get to where we want to go; what restaurants/shops/facilities are nearby; where the nearest bus stop is and when the next bus is arriving; when a shop closes; the identity of the plant or bird we've just seen or the music we are listening to. And much more.

Negatives

You might think that there couldn't be anything wrong with information and knowledge, that being able to find out anything about anything, free or almost free, could only be good. I think there are some interesting and important negatives, including some that affect us on a daily basis, and which will affect the adults around you as much as you.

INFORMATION OVERLOAD – TIREDNESS AND POOR PROCESSING

Do you sometimes have so much information coming in from different sources that you feel anxious and stressed? Or you don't hear what someone is saying because you're already trying to deal with other mental or physical tasks? Or you keep reading the same thing over and over but it doesn't go in because your mind was on something else?

This can happen without being online, of course, but when we are online, it happens a *lot*: headlines, notifications, things to respond or react to, stuff to remember or process, several windows open on our computer, several apps on our phone.

Everything you read or hear – even the most trivial message – requires some concentration, some brain activity. Every time your neurons fire up – in other words, every time you do any mental or physical activity, even something tiny, such as noticing the time – those brain cells use oxygen and energy in the form of glucose. This energy loss will lead to tiredness after a while. The more information you try to process, the more quickly you're going to use up energy and become tired.

We can manage a certain amount of information easily. And we can sometimes manage to take on board extra, even when it's coming at us fast, but we can't keep that up for long. We get tired and can't process things so well. We don't need brain scans to tell us when we have information overload (and a brain scan couldn't exactly tell you that anyway) because we can feel the strain and tiredness. Some people will say, "My brain hurts!" Actually, it doesn't, but your head can hurt and it certainly feels like your brain, rather than your foot.

The information that comes at us is usually a mixture of important (such as an instruction or a fact) and trivial (someone has liked your latest photo, for example). We have to spend some energy working out which is which. And sometimes the more trivial things attract our attention the most because they may be more fun.

If you're learning facts or vocabulary, you know you need to take a few on board at a time, process them and then move on to the next ones. Or if you're trying to read something complicated or work out some maths, you are aware you need to concentrate, and devote the right amount of time to the task. So, you can imagine that if there's just too much else going on in your brain, some things, including important information, may not be processed properly.

HOW TO AVOID THIS NEGATIVE:

1. Recognize the signs that your brain is overloaded and have a rest. If you feel you're becoming tired and less able to concentrate, or what you're reading or listening to isn't going in properly, take a ten-minute break. You don't have to lie down: just do something different, away from your screen.

2. See if there's any information source you can get rid of: any apps you can lose, any notifications you can switch off.

3. When you need to focus on a piece of work, take steps

to close down other windows on your computer or switch off notifications on your phone. Ideally, put the phone on silent and out of sight.

LESS GOOD AT DEEP READING

I mentioned that we might be becoming better at skim-reading. At the same time, it's very possible (and logical) that we may be becoming less good at deep reading. That could matter in two ways: we may not be making the effort to understand difficult text and we may also not bother to process it so deeply because we subconsciously know we can always find it again easily. There's some evidence this may be happening. But it is hard to measure and we probably won't have really good evidence one way or the other. So, just be honest with yourself: do you *think* you are good at reading deeply, focusing on a complex text and sticking with it till you understand it? If this is something you find difficult – and lots of people do – I recommend you follow these tips.

HOW TO AVOID THIS NEGATIVE:

1. Once a day, give yourself time to do some focused reading. It can be work or pleasure reading but it needs to be with your potentially distracting devices off and out of sight. Reading before bed is a good plan. (If you read on an eBook reader, make sure all your social media and other apps that might bring

notifications are switched off.)

2. While you're reading, be aware of where your mind is. If it starts to wander, pull it back on task. If it keeps wandering, get up and go for a short fast walk, even just around the block, have a drink of water and go back to the task. Don't go online or pick your phone up in this break.

3. While you're reading, imagine someone is going to ask you to explain it to them.

4. Set yourself a goal with a time limit: "I will focus hard on this piece of material for fifteen minutes, and at the end of that I will understand it."

5. Don't worry if this doesn't always work: it's a set of skills you're learning and practice will help.

FALSE INFORMATION AND FAKE NEWS

These are two different things. False information includes things that are wrong because the writer made a mistake or interpreted wrongly, or because the science later changes to contradict what we previously thought was true. So it's accidentally wrong. Fake news is when someone deliberately spreads or creates a story that is simply not true. Fake news is a lie, or, at very best, a joke. It is then often shared by people who genuinely believe it. And because the Internet makes it so easy to spread things, and because fake news is designed to be so interesting that many people will believe it, it can spread incredibly fast.

Before the Web, most information was in books or articles written by experts with long training in their subject. Even so, they could be wrong. After all, we still don't know everything, and expert scientists, historians or lawyers can still disagree with each other or learn some new information that proves what they previously believed was right is in fact wrong. They have arguments and debates and sometimes there is no absolute "right" answer.

However, those books and articles had always been through a process of editing and review by other experts, so you could be reasonably sure that what you were reading had a good chance of being right, or at least well supported by some evidence.

Now anyone can write and publish anything and it is much harder for the reader to judge how likely it is to be good quality.

It's very easy for us, at any age, to believe things we want to believe, the stories that fit what we already think. If you dislike a particular person – a celebrity, say – and then you read a shocking story about them, you're likely to believe it. You might even share it, because you find it funny or you think your friends will appreciate it. But what if it's not true? I think that matters. It's a human being at the end of that story. I wouldn't like lies to be spread about me.

But false information and fake news are far more

serious than stories about one person, although that's bad enough because it can be so cruel and damaging to that person. False information and fake news matter because they affect what people think about really important aspects of life, such as climate change, religious extremism, sexual abuse, gender equality, disability, our political leaders; and that can affect how people vote. And that's important. Very important. You don't want fake news to be the structure on which our lives and laws are built.

I want to know the truth about things and I'm sure you do. I want to be able to have a strong opinion on whether our energy needs should come from wind and sun or from nuclear power, or what extra rights or benefits a particular group should have, or which political party should be blamed for what, or whether social media is good or bad for self-esteem and well-being. But I want that opinion to be based on facts, not stuff that someone made up just to persuade me.

The evidence is that we are dealing with this problem really badly. In a 2016 report for the Stanford History Education Group, the authors looked at the ability of thousands of US students to work out the likely truth of various online documents and concluded: "Overall, young people's ability to reason about the information on the Internet can be summed up in one word: *bleak*." Of course, as they pointed out, there were lots of differences and some young people were far better at this than others (and, I'd add, many adults are pretty bad at it, too), but they said: "At present, we worry that democracy is threatened by the ease at which disinformation about civic issues is allowed to spread and flourish."

HOW TO AVOID THIS NEGATIVE:

1. Value the truth and want to find it. Your arguments will be so much stronger if you know that what you're saying is true.

2. When you read anything online, ask why you should believe it. Adults sometimes lie, and they often get things wrong! See below for my lists of reasons to trust and distrust what you read.

3. Don't share until you're sure. And if you discover later that you were misled, say so. It happens to us all.

4. Remember that there are usually two sides to a story. Try to see it from the other side to see if you've missed anything.

5. Never just read the headline and first few lines. Read the whole thing: you'll often find the rest of the article says something quite different.

6. Use your head and then your heart when evaluating information.

Reasons to Trust

- The website is run by a large, well-known charity or government organization.

- The website is run by an organization that is not trying to sell something.
- The information is also in a book which was published by a publisher who's independent of the author.
- The author has a reputation on this subject and you have good reason to believe that they have genuine expertise.
- The research that you are reading about was conducted by a university or an organization which is not trying to sell something.
- The research has been supported by other research and is not just one tiny study that hasn't yet been checked.
- An Internet search reveals lots of sensible-sounding people who seem to agree with what you're reading.

Reasons to Distrust

(One of these things alone doesn't suggest a problem...)
- The headline and opening sentences don't match the rest of the article. Never assume that the headline is the whole story. Read the whole article, as you'll often find the middle and end are very different from the start.
- The story has a "clickbait" heading. These are stories that urge you to click on them but all they

want is for you to see the adverts. Those "15 things you didn't know about XXX Celebrity" are classic clickbait.

- The research was carried out by a company that stands to gain. So, research by a chocolate company showing that chocolate is good for you is less trustworthy than research by an independent organization.
- The story has come from a person or organization that you already know is biased.
- The story looks like a news story but is actually an advertisement – sometimes there's the phrase "advertising feature" in tiny print.
- The story has not been picked up by the national newspapers in your country.
- On Facebook and other social media sites, any "sponsored posts". I'm not saying they're all untrue or fake, but they are paid-for advertising and there's only one reason for them: to sell something.

BIASED SEARCH RESULTS

Google and other search engines want to give you what they think you want. They notice what you search for and they make judgements about what you like and how you think. Then, when you search for something, they filter the results so that you see the ones that are likely to interest you most. Google knows that we humans are all somewhat biased and want to read what fits our world view. And Google tries to give us that.

Imagine two people, one called Joe and one called Ellie. They both spend time online. They both have different interests but one they share is an interest in the environment. Joe wants to go into farming so he reads a lot of information from farming organizations and he's been investigating various organic methods for farming cattle and pigs. Ellie lives on a riverboat on a city canal, is a vegan and an activist for humane treatment of animals. One evening, they both happen to do a Google search for the phrase "organic ethical humane farming". The results they get are very different. Google knows what organizations and topics they both spend most time on and gives them material that fits their habits.

This means that, although they are both happy because they get what they are looking for, they are unlikely to find things that challenge their views. Not enough people go searching for their views to be challenged, and, if they do, they won't usually find that on Google.

I think it's important for our views to be challenged. If there's another side to the argument, we should know it. Not to weaken our position but to allow us to strengthen it if we can.

HOW TO AVOID THIS NEGATIVE:

1. Be aware of it. Realize that you are not being offered

an unbiased selection. You have biased the selection yourself, without meaning to, because Google judges you based on what you've done or looked at online.

2. If you hold a particular belief or opinion, make an effort to find and read the other side of the story. Search engines are not *hiding* the other side; they are just offering you what you believe in first. It's up to you to find the counter-argument.

ACCESS TO PORNOGRAPHY

The truth is, we don't know how many young people access porn or how often, or at what age, because the figures you see widely quoted are based on what young people say, and there are all sorts of reasons why they might not tell the truth. What we do know is that Internet porn is a whole different world from the top-shelf magazines of a generation ago. Much of the imagery is incredibly violent and disturbing, using rape as a regular theme, and including child abuse. So if you do get your information about sex from online porn you'll be getting an extremely warped, wrong and unhealthy view of it. Anyone who gets their information from porn would think that consent was not necessary, that violence was normal or acceptable, that women are objects, that pain is desirable, and that love and respect play no part in sex. And those things are deeply, dangerously untrue. Pornography is *not* sex. If you do it like that, you're doing it wrong.

Many adults worry that watching Internet porn is warping the views of both boys and girls about relationships. They also worry about boys becoming addicted to online porn and not being able to form healthy relationships of their own and having sexual dysfunction later. There have been cases of this, and some countries have seen a rise in sexual offences committed by young people.

But we don't know the extent to which watching porn has this effect. There could be other causes behind the problems we find. Fortunately, most young people don't get their sex education exclusively from porn – they also learn from school, family, each other, and good quality online resources.

We do know that young people report being upset and disturbed by some of the images they see. And once you've seen something, you can't unsee it.

HOW TO AVOID THIS NEGATIVE:

1. The simple answer is not to watch porn, ever. Then you'll be safe from the disturbing, violent, false pictures it portrays.
2. If you do see it, don't share it. It could be illegal. Delete it from your phone or other devices. Delete your browsing history.
3. If you see anything you don't understand or are disturbed by, talk to someone you trust.

4. If someone asks you to watch it, you don't have to. Just say you're not interested; you don't like abuse; you think it's ridiculous – anything you want.

5. Always remember that sex should be with mutual consent – that means both parties, equally. No violence; no force; no one doing anything they don't want to do. Don't fall into the trap of thinking that what you see is "right".

6. Also remember that the models used in porn videos or images are just that: models, actors. All sorts of clever filming techniques and make-up are used to make them look the way they do. They are not natural but artificial in shape, hairlessness and many aspects of their appearance.

Summing Up

The access to information on the Web is phenomenal, amazing, brilliant. I love it. It has changed my life. And it's changed yours, compared to the lives of teenagers a generation ago. But we all have to be careful to make sure we don't exhaust ourselves, wreck our concentration and allow ourselves to believe false information. We need to make good judgements about what we allow into our heads.

Resources

Daniel J. Levitin, in his book, *The Organized Mind: Thinking Straight in the Age of Information Overload* (2014), quotes figures to show how much data we deal with now. There are many citations in his end-notes, to lead you to what interests you.

Levitin refers to work by Roger E. Bohn and James E. Short and you can see their report, "How Much Information? 2009 Report on American Consumers," at **www.researchgate.net/publication/242562463_How_Much_Information)2009_Report_on_American_Consumers**

"How Much Data Is Created on the Internet Each Day?" by Jeff Shultz has some startling statistics at **https://blog.microfocus.com/how-much-data-is-created-on-the-internet-each-day/**

Evidence that we may be becoming less good at deep reading can be found in this 2010 article, "Google Generation II: web behaviour experiments with the BBC", by David Nicholas, Ian Rowlands, David Clark and Peter Williams: **pdfs.semanticscholar.org/a3e0/75d194661568b6279ed82ac1641576ce9c4f.pdf**

There is useful insight into false information and fake news in Tim Lott's 2016 article, "How do I tell my daughter that her online 'truth' is a conspiracy theory?", at **www.theguardian.com/lifeandstyle/2016/nov/11/truth-conspiracy-theory-internet-online-children?CMP=Share_iOSApp_Other**

The Stanford History Education Group's 2016 research paper, "Evaluating Information: The cornerstone of civic online reasoning", by Sam Wineburg, Sarah McGrew, Joel Breakstone and Teresa Ortega, can be found at **www.purl.stanford.edu/ fv751yt5934** There is also a shorter report on this at **www. ed.stanford.edu/news/stanford-researchers-find-students-have-trouble-judging-credibility-information-online**

The effects of porn are discussed in The Sexualization Report, edited by Feona Attwood, Clare Bale and Meg Barker in 2013: **www.thesexualizationreport.wordpress.com/4-young-people-sex/is-pornography-dangerous-for-young-people/**

Sonia Livingstone, Professor of Social Psychology at the LSE in the UK, argues in the article, "No, the Internet is not actually stealing kids' innocence" (2017), that the dangers of the Internet have been exaggerated: **http://blogs.lse.ac.uk/ parenting4digitalfuture/2017/08/16/no-the-internet-is-not-actually-stealing-kids-innocence/**

Busy Brains: Active and Alert

Life online keeps our brains busy: active and learning, alert to opportunities, wide awake. Sounds good. Like the body, the brain responds well to being used and exercised. We are stimulating our brains in many different ways, learning new skills, absorbing more information, opening our minds to new possibilities, keeping mentally active, rarely being bored.

Activity is good, right? As with most things, there are positives and negatives.

Positives

EXERCISING OUR BRAINS

Different online activities use different brain areas. So, whether we're reading information, doing rapid messaging with several groups of friends at once, watching YouTube videos, gaming, sharing photos or status updates, or whatever, we are certainly exercising areas of our brain.

This means we are mentally alert while we are doing these things and we know that being mentally alert is good for people of all ages. There's plenty of evidence that having an active mind can help prevent dementia (though there's no evidence that online is better than offline mental activity, and the research usually focuses on activities such as doing a crossword or learning a second language).

NO NEED TO BE BORED

It's now possible never to be bored! My childhood was full of times when I'd moan, "Mum, I'm BORED!" Now we don't have to be bored, because there's always something we can do on our phones or other devices. Entertainment and activity are on demand.

LEARNING NEW SKILLS

While we are exercising our brains, taking all these opportunities from the screens in front of us, we are likely to be improving certain skills.

Depending on what we're doing, we could be improving our reaction speeds or our ability to notice moving objects at the side of our vision, being creative, practising hand to eye coordination. We might be learning facts and storing them in our memory; developing empathy and understanding of people who are different; improving our writing, art, coding, design, film-making skills. We could be finding inspiration for new careers or directions for our lives.

DIGITAL TOOLS FOR OUR MEMORY

A human's memory is pretty huge and we won't run out

of space in our long-term memory, but there is a limit to how much we can store in short- and medium-term memory. Facts like what your homework is, shopping lists, what you have to do this evening, what you need to remember to take to football or swimming, phone numbers or social media names, groups you belong to, things you'd like for Christmas: all these things can now be recorded in your phone, either by you taking a photo or making a note. You don't have to use any memory space or brain bandwidth for them. Often the lists sync across your devices, making them extra useful.

Also, when you've found some information, you don't have to focus on remembering it, because you can always find it again. You can bookmark web pages, save it to a note app, or just Google it again.

So you can have more brain space for thinking, for understanding, for talking, for anything else, because you're not using valuable brain bandwidth for some short-term memory items.

Negatives

This is an area where the negatives have the widest effect, in my view. Many people won't suffer the negatives involved in things like self-esteem or trolling or addictive use, but no one is immune to all the negatives I'm going to suggest now.

DISTRACTION AND LOSS OF CONCENTRATION

Information overload affects our concentration. When we're trying to focus on a task and other information comes in, it is distracting. You know that from your own experience. Maybe you're engrossed in a computer game, or you're trying to work out a maths problem, or you're reading for pleasure: if someone interrupts to tell or ask you something, your thinking is disrupted and it can take a while to get back.

When you're online or working on a screen, that happens a lot. Think about this scenario and see if it rings a bell. You're using your laptop to go online to investigate something for homework. You've found a good website and you're reading the information. On the screen are many distractions: down the sidebars, there are adverts and icons, links to other websites; some of the adverts or icons are moving or brightly coloured. These are all tempting; they are all making you think, "Maybe I should click on this, in case there's something more interesting or exciting through that link." We are programmed to be distracted and curious, remember.

You may also have your social media windows open behind the website you're on. And notifications may come from them. More temptations, decisions, distractions.

"That's OK," you may say. "I can resist those temptations."

Maybe you can. But be careful: resisting temptation takes a lot of brain bandwidth and energy. You will lose a little bit of time and focus. This might not matter if it only happens occasionally but if you have to do it lots of times while engaged on one piece of work, that would add up and it might matter.

Psychologist Linda Stone came up with the phrase "continuous partial attention" to describe the state that many of us find ourselves in often: the feeling that we're rarely fully engaged on a task, but flitting between tasks. I know the feeling!

But can't we multitask? Learn to do it better? Apparently not. It's possible that there may be a small number of people (one study suggests about 2% but I'm not convinced by the research, which seems to test a very specific task that bears little relation to real life) who genuinely perform better when competing information is coming at them. But for the rest of us, our brains work on a simple bandwidth principle: like a broadband connection, we have a fixed processing speed or capacity for conscious activities; everything we do occupies some bandwidth, some things a little and others a lot. And when we are using a moderate amount on one task, other tasks are slowed down or become impossible.

Some people have suggested that people of your generation, "digital natives" who have grown up with the online world, may be better at dealing with this distraction and therefore better at multitasking. The evidence, I'm afraid, is that the opposite is more likely to be true! The thing is that yes, we tend to become better at what we spend lots of time on, and digital natives have usually grown up spending lots of time being distracted and not focusing on one thing at a time. So, you are likely to be very good at ... being distracted and not focusing on one thing at a time! But being genuinely good at multitasking means being able to concentrate on more than one thing at once and to perform well on a core task when being distracted by other things. All we are doing when we allow distractions is not actually focusing on one thing at all and therefore not performing well on the task in hand.

Does background music spoil concentration? Good question! According to what I've just said, listening to music while working *ought* to be a bad idea, because part of your brain is occupied with the music. And I'll admit the research isn't clear. But here's what I tell teachers, parents and teenagers, having read a lot of the research on both sides: there's good reason to believe that having background music, chosen by you, while you work may help you concentrate. It seems that having something that occupies only a tiny amount of brain bandwidth, because you're not really concentrating on it, can help trigger you to use all the rest of your concentration on the task. Also, and more simply, it can do a very good job of blocking out the irritating noises that really could be distracting you.

I'd suggest you ask yourself one question: which would be less distracting, familiar music that makes me feel good or the noises made by traffic, your family or your classmates? I reckon that's a vote for music.

Having said that, I think there are some things to consider first to make sure this works for you: the music needs to be very familiar, as anything new is going to distract you more; you need to create a playlist in advance so that you don't have to stop when you come to a track you don't like; make sure the volume is not too intrusive; and it may be better to choose music without lyrics. Experiment with different music to see what you genuinely feel is helping you.

HOW TO AVOID THIS NEGATIVE:

1. Realize that you *will* feel and function better if you minimize distractions. Whenever possible, switch off software you're not using.

2. When you need to focus on something important, switch other devices off. Tell yourself you're now in focus mode until the job is done.

3. Keep your devices out of sight when you're not using them.

4. Investigate programmes that help you switch off or block distracting social media apps when you're working. I won't recommend any as they keep changing, but you'll easily find a free one.

5. Follow the Pomodoro technique. This involves setting

a timer (can be an alarm clock, or a Pomodoro app or whatever) for a certain time – ideally twenty-five minutes, as this is not too daunting – and switching off or blocking all notifications and social media sites (again, there are apps to block them for you); you then focus on your piece of work till the timer rings. It's remarkably empowering!

6. Write your task or target down and have it where you can see it. You can reward yourself when it's done.

7. Always notice how you feel when you have managed to switch off distractions. Enjoy it!

EXHAUSTION

Of course, any activity, whether mental or physical, uses energy and is therefore tiring. No one has endless energy and everyone works less well when exhausted. Don't let your energy levels drop too far: they moderate your activity with the right amount of rest and fuel.

HOW TO AVOID THIS NEGATIVE:

1. Simple: make sure you have plenty of breaks from technology! Have a break every hour at least, and when you start to feel your concentration flagging.

2. Remember that we tend to get more tired if we keep doing the same thing for too long, so a simple change of task can help. If you've been on a screen for a long time, do something off screen.

BUT BOREDOM IS A GOOD THING, TOO!

I offered "no need to be bored" as a positive, but there is a negative attached to it. Although we might not enjoy that feeling of boredom, and although being bored can make us do silly or negative things (such as snacking or risk-taking), there's evidence that periods of nothing to do can be mentally useful.

I think it depends what we mean by boredom. A long period of boredom, or feeling bored with your life, not being able to find meaning – those things are unpleasant but are not really what I'm talking about here. I'm talking about short periods of having nothing to do and not knowing what to do. These are the periods of time that we tend to avoid by getting out our phones immediately. It's as though we are afraid of an empty minute or ten.

These short periods of nothingness are what may be valuable, even necessary. Particularly if you want to be in any way original, creative, proactive, instead of just following everyone else.

It's these periods of boredom or "non-busyness" that can allow daydreaming, and daydreaming has good evidence to support its value, at least if that daydreaming is deliberate.

Many people knew this instinctively before any research was done. Highly creative people have talked about the value of being alone and without activity. The writer Franz Kafka said: "Remain sitting at your table and listen. You need not even listen, simply wait, just learn to become quiet, still and solitary. The world will freely offer itself to you to be unmasked." The American writer Robert Pirsig said "Boredom always precedes a period of great creativity." Mozart and Picasso both talked of valuing solitude and quiet.

Now we have studies that support this in different ways. Research suggests that periods of boredom or having nothing specific to focus on help us think creatively. Many people notice that it's when we are not busy and not actively thinking about something that the best ideas come. The word "composting" has been used to describe what happens in our brain when we've been thinking about something or working on a problem and then we stop to do something that requires little thinking; later we have a brilliant solution or thought. I and many writers I know find that we often get stuck while looking at the screen and if we go for a walk and let our thoughts wander the ideas become unblocked.

It's when we haven't got anything specific to do – when we allow ourselves not to fill that space by picking up our phone – that we think of new ideas or work out problems. Everyone needs that space to fill with dreams, hopes, ambitions, solutions. If we eat without stopping, we can't digest our food; if we feed our brain without stopping, we can't process our thoughts.

But this is not an excuse for daydreaming all day! It

seems that the ideal is to mix periods of concentration with periods of unfocused thought or daydreaming.

HOW TO AVOID THIS NEGATIVE:

1. Don't be afraid of empty times. Don't feel you have to fill them with entertainment or contact with other people.
2. Actively seek and embrace these empty times. Give yourself a fifteen-minute daydream time every day. See what ideas come.
3. Sometimes, put your phone away. Go into the garden without it. Go to the park and sit on a swing, without your phone. Lie on the grass and do nothing.
4. Alternate daydreaming time with focused activity.
5. Nurture the skill of being alone. It's an excellent and useful skill to have as there are bound to be times in your life when you're on your own. Learn to love it!

Summing Up

I think it stands to reason that being busy and active, whether physically or mentally, is going to have benefits and disadvantages. It's obviously good to be active: it makes us stronger, more skilled, more alert. But it's equally important not to overdo it and to allow ourselves enough rest. Importantly, we should not feel guilty about taking breaks, as those breaks are necessary for our wellbeing and performance.

Resources

Linda Stone explains "continuous partial attention" on her website at **www.lindastone.net/qa/continuous-partial-attention/**

For more discussion on multi-tasking, see Christian Jarrett's 2015 article, "How the Brains of 'Super-Multitaskers' are Different", at **www.nymag.com/scienceofus/2015/05/brains-of-super-multitaskers-are-different.html**

You can read "The Disturbing Facts About Digital Natives" by Paul A. Kirschner (2015) on the 3-Star Learning Experiences blog at **www.3starlearningexperiences.wordpress.com/2015/10/20/the-disturbing-facts-about-digital-natives/**

"Tiny distractions can double mistakes" is an interesting article on the effect of distractions, by Tia Ghose in *Scientific American Mind* (2013): **www.scientificamerican.com/article/tiny-distractions-can-double/**

I wrote "Can you work well while listening to music?" at **www.nicolamorgan.com/heartsong-blog/can-you-work-well-while-listening-to-music/**

Bradley Busch highlights research that disagrees in his article "Drowned in sound: how listening to music hinders learning" (2018): **www.theguardian.com/teacher-network/2018/mar/14/sound-how-listening-music-hinders-learning-lessons-research** (This research doesn't account for any beneficial effect of music in countering annoying distractions, such as unwanted noise.)

Joseph Stromberg's article "The Benefits of Daydreaming" (2012) discusses the advantages of boredom: **www. smithsonianmag.com/science-nature/the-benefits-of-daydreaming-170189213/**

Simon Moesgaard-Kjeldsen discusses different daydream styles in his article "There Are 3 Different 'Styles' of Daydreaming" (2013) at **www.businessinsider.com/different-types-of-daydreaming-2013-9?IR=T**

In "Boredom is Good For You", published in The Atlantic (2017), Jude Stewart refers to several studies suggesting specific benefits to daydreaming: **www.tandfonline.com/doi/abs/10.10 80/10400419.2014.901073#.VNL8MWTF98s**

The Internet and Creativity

Humans are very creative beings. Even small children love to make things – mud pies, sand castles, pictures, funny songs, new words – and as we get older we take pride and pleasure when we make something with tools, written or spoken words, pictures, design, music and song, photos, film. We have ideas in our heads and we like to try to turn them into reality, even if the result isn't quite what we imagined. Sometimes we do it for pleasure, sometimes as a job or to earn money, and sometimes for both. When we spend lots of time on one type of creative skill, we get better at it and more experienced, and the things we create give more pleasure, to ourselves and often to other people.

That desire to create things hasn't changed with the new online world. But the tools and how we can learn and share our creations have changed enormously. There's no doubt that there are major positives from the Internet and everything on it, but there may well be some negatives.

Positives

DEMONSTRATIONS EVERYWHERE!

Whatever you want to learn to do, there's always a stack of demo videos on YouTube. OK, lots of them are terrible, but the best usually go to the top of the search results and it's not too difficult to find a good one. So, whether you want to know how to use a new piece of art software, create an animation using pipe-cleaner figures, grow sunflowers or ice a cake to look like a dinosaur, someone out there has demonstrated it and put the video on the Internet, free for anyone to watch.

Each type of creativity – painting, writing, making music etc. – has whole websites devoted to it, with high quality demonstrations and questions and answers from other enthusiasts.

Apart from the more ordinary skills, there are also some astonishing videos of creativity in action: incredible ice or sand sculptures, street or pavement art, glass-blowing, dances, acrobatics. While they might not exactly teach you how to imitate the creation, they can be incredibly inspiring.

COMMUNITY

I mentioned that any art or craft or hobby will have websites devoted to it. This also means that you can engage and chat with lots of other people who are enthusiastic about the same thing. And generally people are really willing to share and support each other. That's one of the joys of the Internet.

So, if you love creating pictures with pancake batter (that is a Thing!), want to make a quilt for your aunt who's in hospital, want to get better at calligraphy, or are into carving wooden figures or making animations, there are people out there who can help you, encourage you and welcome you. You can all share your knowledge and enthusiasm.

NEW TOOLS AND SHORTCUTS

Although many artists would say that nothing beats the act of creating a picture using traditional brushes and paints, you can create wonderful results using software on your computer or tablet. And you don't need to have spent years practising your art to get to a stage where you can create something satisfying. Difficult skills like perspective in drawing, editing video, or recording music are much easier with technology.

Artist David Hockney famously embraced digital technology, using an iPad to create a whole new range of work. And many professional artists use digital technology – both hardware and software – to extend their range or develop particular styles. So it's something worth recognizing as a benefit. (Though I do have something to say about this in the section on negatives.)

Many of these tools allow you to create things that would take a very long time by hand. For example, using a Pointillist style, which builds a picture out of individual tiny dots, becomes easy with software; and you can create a watercolour or oil effect without going to the trouble of getting out your watercolours or oils (though some would say that the "trouble" is part of the pleasure and the process!). Artists I know often do the drawing by hand but then fill in the colour digitally because it's quicker.

Techniques such as animation or 3D design would be difficult or impossible to achieve without digital tools, and those tools can allow you to create a particular look or style – such as a vintage or retro look – that would be much harder to create from scratch unless it was something you'd practised for ages. So you can be more versatile and experimental. That's good.

INFORMATION, MATERIALS AND TIPS

Manufacturers are always developing new physical tools, whether brushes, paints, paper, lenses, baking or cooking gadgets, or any of the infinite items you might need for whatever creative thing you're into. The Internet allows you to know about these easily. Many of the websites for each craft are funded by advertising or selling these items (so always think carefully before buying, of course), but my point is that you'll find out about these things in a way you might not have done before the Internet. You'll find people raving about a particular sort of paint or a new smartphone app, and you'll see examples of it being used and be able to decide whether it's right for you.

Also, you can check the quality or usefulness of something by reading the reviews. So, suppose someone is advertising a new piece of software that apparently creates amazing animations; you can find reviews from people who've used it and who have discovered the advantages and disadvantages.

NO WASTE OR MESS!

An artist friend of mine said of working digitally: "Endless adjustments and no messy cleaning up ... what could be better?" (He did also contribute quite a few negative comments, as you'll see!) But yes, you don't have to buy loads of materials and occupy the whole kitchen with your mess, spend hours tidying up, or waste a forest of paper.

NO BARRIERS

One of the best things about all this is that people of any age can produce wonderful creations online. You don't have to have left school before you can have your words, art, music or films published. The playing field is much more level than before the Internet.

You don't need to be rich to access the tools, either. Having said that, it is still true – and unfair – that people at the poorest end of the scale do have great difficulty accessing a decent computer and smartphone, so it's not true to say that everyone can use these opportunities.

But you don't need to have gone to art school, go to expensive classes or be one of the best writers or artists in your school in order to develop many artistic skills. So, although, yes, you do need access to a computer and some people struggle with this, it's a more open playing field than in the days when the only routes to being creative were to have either a private hobby or to have a career in that field.

The Internet is relatively democratic and accessible. It opens doors: not all doors and not to everyone, but more than in the past. Opportunities are wider, thanks to the Internet and the Web.

THE CHANCE TO BE FAMOUS

It's hard to talk about online fame without mentioning Zoella. And that is her second mention in this book! So, yes, Zoella, Joe Sugg, Alfie Deyes and a load of others you'll know more about than I do have all become very famous – and very wealthy – very young, simply through doing stuff on the Internet. Stuff which many other people have tried to do – perhaps because it doesn't look difficult – but which very few people will succeed at, or at least in terms of that amount of success. My point is the Internet gives everyone a chance to be famous but it's like giving everyone a lottery ticket: you have a chance to win, but most people won't.

Of course, below the level of the most famous, there are thousands of people – and many of them are young – who have done something really well and become well known or respected for it.

FREE SHOWCASE FOR YOUR CREATIONS

Before the Internet, if you'd written a story or painted a picture, carved a wooden bowl or made some earrings, you had very few options if you wanted to let other people see or buy your creation. You had to persuade a publisher, find a gallery to take a risk on your painting, or a craft fair to sell your wooden bowl or earrings. The hurdles were high and it was very difficult to do anything with your creations other than let your family and friends admire them. That is a very good start and there is *nothing* wrong with creating things just for yourself and people you know. But now, there are many more options.

For your written work, you might use Wattpad, as very many young writers do and where you can get feedback. Or you can create your own blog, making it public or private. You could publish your poems, stories and even your novel and sell them via Amazon, Lulu, CreateSpace. I should warn you that it's not easy to sell, and there are some downsides as I'll mention in the section on negatives, but it's possible and not complicated.

You can create a website of your own where you can

display your artwork. You can sell your crafts on websites such as Etsy. You can publish your videos and animations on YouTube. You can showcase your music and singing on Spotify, iTunes, SoundCloud. Whatever your creative direction, there's somewhere online where you can show it to the world, or, if you prefer, just to select people.

Since I didn't know much about putting artwork online, of course I did an Internet search and the results I got are a really good example of how the Internet allows us to discover things: in the first page of results were not only several sites and articles listing hundreds of possibilities but also an article about the things you should know before selling your art online. So, there you have a great example that, although the Internet is often a scarily huge place where people are trying to sell you things or take advantage of you, it's also a place where, if you keep your eyes open, there are lots of people trying to make sure no one is ripped off. If I really wanted to sell my art online, I'd look at the helpful warning stories first and try to get the best and most trustworthy advice from a site not trying to sell me something and from people who've actually done what I'm interested in.

This is where I really do need to ask you to look at the negatives before getting too excited about the definite positives. I want you to be able to experience the joy of controlling your own creation, rather than anyone to take advantage of you.

Negatives

GOING PUBLIC BEFORE YOU'RE READY

Recently I came across the manuscript of the first book I wrote, which was never published. I started reading it and was incredibly glad that it hadn't been! My writing wasn't ready; I wasn't good enough. But in the years when I was failing to be published, self-publishing wasn't an option. Would I have been tempted down that route? I don't know. But I know I'd have regretted it.

Just because something is easy to do doesn't make it the best thing to do. And I think there are times when it's better to keep practising, keep working to become better and better and to be as sure as possible that you really do want your work read, your art seen or your music heard by the general public.

Of course, it's great that there are so many ways to show your creations and to get feedback – positive and negative – so I'm *not* saying don't do it. I'm just saying that putting your work out too soon could certainly be seen as a negative.

The writer Terry Pratchett once said that after his death all the unpublished or unfinished works on his computer hard drive should be crushed under a steamroller. He knew they weren't ready; he wasn't happy enough with them. I would do the same.

Creative people should have control over their work

and that includes controlling when people get to see it. "Creative people" includes you: anyone who creates something, whether teenage or adult, whether amateur, hobbyist or professional, has rights over what happens to something they've created.

HOW TO AVOID THIS NEGATIVE:

1. Think carefully before you put anything you've created online. Try to look ahead to how you might feel later, when perhaps you've improved even more. Of course, it's hard to look ahead and I wouldn't want you to be afraid to do anything, but I'm just saying: try to act thoughtfully.

2. Get a second opinion from someone you trust, to see if there's anything you haven't thought about or anything you'd like to change.

3. See if there's any advice online about how to publicize whatever type of thing you've created, and learn about the pitfalls first.

4. Remember that it's there for ever. In theory, you can remove or delete things you've put on the Internet if you change your mind, but it's not always easy and sometimes it's too late. If it's been copied or shared, you've lost control. Again, this doesn't mean don't do it, just that you need to know the downsides.

MISSING IMPORTANT SKILLS

Think about those art apps and tools I mentioned under Positives, all the things that make it so much easier to "draw" or "paint" something that looks wonderful, without going to art classes or learning how to create it from scratch. All that is great if it's just a hobby for you or if you are satisfied with the result, but what if you want to be a professional artist of some sort? Is it enough that you can use the software? Will you feel inadequate or dissatisfied when you see people who've learnt to produce the effects purely by hand?

Since this isn't my area of knowledge, I asked two artist friends, both of whom not only work professionally and successfully as artists but who also teach in schools and in a leading art college, so they come across many artists of their own age but also much younger. They both use digital media, and both were absolutely certain that they got extra pleasure from creating directly onto paper with handheld tools and "real" paint or whatever. They also said that having the background skills gives them power and control over their art. It allows them to experiment, break rules, feel really creative. They use digital media to do something extra or to do a more boring task more quickly, but it seems that nothing beats the truly hands-on process of creation.

The one who has most eagerly embraced technology said: "You can look like an amazing designer but, in fact, you are just cutting and pasting the work of real designers. Your work looks cool, because it's the current meme template, but it's like junk food and ultimately unsatisfying, though brilliant for the fast meme culture we live in, where it only needs to look cool for a day or two." And: "I did quite a few series drawing digitally until I got so bored I went back to the pen again, which is so much more satisfying." He did say he was "sure it's different if you have been brought up a native digital artist".

Maybe that is true. But it still means you haven't learnt certain basic skills and I think that would hold you back if you wanted art to be your career. (Though I also believe it's never too late to learn.)

HOW TO AVOID THIS NEGATIVE:

1. If you want to do art as a career or take it more seriously than a hobby, try not to take shortcuts when it comes to learning skills. It may take time to learn a strong skill but it could well be worth it. You will never regret learning something.
2. Enjoy being creative. Enjoy the process. Enjoy learning. Enjoy improving.

LACK OF ORIGINALITY

I guess art (including writing and all forms of creation) begins with copying and influence. I remember tracing over pictures as a child and feeling that it was helping me learn to draw for myself. The Internet brings us lots of ways to copy – whether by using software for art or the various fan-fiction sites.

There's nothing wrong with this type of copying for personal practice, development or fun (as long as you don't pretend it's your own work), but the art college lecturer made this point: "Much of what I see young illustrators do is imitative of the culture they grew up in. Some students will be very manga influenced; others fall under the Disney spell. The problem for them is, without strong skills, they haven't the ability or confidence to escape from the generic 'style' they have relied on to be creators. An illustrator's true visual language should come from how they make marks and see the world, not be a pastiche of other image-makers. This for me is a greater problem than not fully grasping perspective. I see too much 'ripping off' and with digital media that has become even easier."

HOW TO AVOID THIS NEGATIVE:

1. Just be aware of the influences you're under. All artists are influenced and there's nothing wrong with it, but it's something to be aware of and not to be trapped by.
2. Again, if you want to be a professional writer or artist one day, don't take shortcuts when it comes to learning skills and developing your style.

3. Spend time looking at the work of many different artists, whether of written or spoken words, or visual arts and crafts.

IS IT REAL?

Again from the field of art (because the conversation with my artist friends was fascinating!), the art college lecturer said: "I find digital art lacks the humanity, the experimentation, the texture, the reality, of handcrafted images. As I teasingly say to my students who rely totally on digital platforms: 'You do realize your art doesn't exist, don't you?' Of course, they can print their images. But who wants to see an exhibition of digital prints of work by, say, Rembrandt? I'd always want to see the wept-over, struggled with, loved/hated and blood, sweat and tears original."

Of course, it's art, even if it's not "real" in the sense of being something you can touch, something that the artists breathed and struggled and sweated over. It can still be skilful, beautiful, mesmerizing, original, thought-provoking and all the other things art can be.

But, although I said it's there for ever, in some ways it's not there at all (until you print it), and it can be lost with a careless click of the wrong button.

HOW TO AVOID THIS NEGATIVE:

1. I think it's just a matter of awareness rather than something to avoid. Again, it makes a difference how seriously you want to take your creativity: hobby or profession, pastime or life?

2. Realize that, although what you've created now seems very real and permanent, you will forget it unless you make it properly permanent. Keep copies or, print things out if appropriate, take photos, keep records. When you're much older, you'll love looking back on what you did.

EASY TO STEAL

I mentioned that copying for practice or fun is fine as long as you don't pretend you didn't copy. But it is very easy for people to steal your work or for you to accidentally break the law and steal someone else's. (And doing it accidentally is no excuse.) The laws of copyright are on the one hand simple: don't use someone else's words or images unless they say you can, and don't pass them off as your own; and yet also complicated: they're different in different countries and it's often hard to decide what is illegal copying and what is lawful quoting or fair use. I'm not going to go into the details here, other than to say: creativity is about creating something new. Be proud of what you create and only be proud of what you created yourself. You can take someone else's idea (there's no copyright on ideas or titles) but you have to turn it into something of your own.

HOW TO AVOID THIS NEGATIVE:

1. Take whatever steps you can to retain control of your creation. For words, images and film, use the copyright symbol – © – and the year you created the item, with your name. You don't have to do this but it's a good way of identifying that you are the owner and people need your permission to use it.

2. Check the copyright laws in your own country, as they are not all the same. Make sure you know your rights and your responsibilities to others.

3. Respect the copyright of others. Ask if you want to use something, even a photo you want to put on a blog. Many people will let you use it for free. Note: "royalty free" does not mean "free" – it means that you pay for it once and don't have to pay each time you use it.

4. Don't put your art on social media if you want to retain control and ownership. Platforms such as Twitter, Instagram and Facebook state that they own the rights to use images and, even if they don't, many people will see images there and believe it's fair to use them themselves. If you're not happy about that, don't put them there, or at least include a very clear © statement.

THERE ARE SHARKS OUT THERE

You may well like the idea of your work being published. Lots of people will offer to help but the important thing to realize is that any company offering to get your work "out there" and publish you without *paying you* is likely to exist to make money out of you and very unlikely to help you sell your work properly.

One such rip-off can happen with a competition where the prize is publication in a book. This *can* be genuine and fine, but there have been examples where parents have received a letter saying something like, "Congratulations! Your son/daughter has won a writing competition and will be published in *blah* book", only to find first that they have to buy copies of the very expensive book and second that the huge majority (or all) of the competition entries were selected. It's lovely to think of your story being in a book but it's also a very easy way for someone to make money: get children to write stories, publish most of them and ask parents to pay more than the actual cost of the book. Nice profit for the organizers but parents and children feel cheated. Of course, anyone is allowed to make money and I've nothing against profit, but are they making money out of you or are they trying to run a decent business that pays its staff and bills? Is it easy money for them or are they really trying to improve young people's creativity? Do they provide lots of good quality free advice or is it all about the "competition"?

HOW TO AVOID THIS NEGATIVE:

1. Remember that being published should cost you nothing and a publisher should pay you. Publishing

something yourself on Amazon is free, apart from the fact that you pay them a bit of commission when you sell a copy.

2. If any website offers to help you be published, check it out on a forum such as Absolute Write. Use the Internet to search for any negative reports about the website.

3. Literary agents do *not* charge anything for considering your work. If they like the look of it, they'll talk to you about it; if they don't, they will usually tell you quickly.

4. If something seems too good to be true, it probably is. Ask an adult, such as a teacher, to check it for you.

5. If you put anything on a website that isn't yours, check that they will not take the copyright or your "moral rights". Copyright is yours – keep it – and moral rights mean that your name must always be attached and that no one can alter the text or artwork without your permission.

6. Check the terms of any competitions you enter. Who judges them? Are they genuine or is this simply a way for the organizers to make easy money? Is the cost small or large?

7. If you and maybe some of your friends – or your whole class – want to self-publish your work, do it! Create a book, design a cover and publish it on Amazon or Lulu, and sell it to whoever would like to buy it.

8. Look at the website of the UK Society of Authors for lots of free advice about publishing, self-publishing and how not to be ripped off.

Summing Up

Although I may have listed more negatives than positives, I think the negatives are actually relatively minor. The online world has a huge amount to offer, with so many exciting and accessible opportunities to be creative. I am in awe of people of all ages who do incredible things with video, art, music, words, drama, dance, and infinite physical and imaginative creativity. I love the fact that age is no barrier and young people can teach older people so much.

Use the opportunities boldly and with a sense of excitement and adventure; enjoy your growing creativity; and be proud of what you can learn to do online. But always remember: make the online world your tool and not your tyrant.

Resources

Your library will have local opportunities for writing, art, drama and crafts. And, of course, you'll find YouTube videos for every kind of creative activity.

Publishing House is a website for young writers, artists and thinkers: **www.publishinghouse.me.uk**

TeenInk is a website written by teens for teens: **www.teenink. com**

Wattpad is a well-known site for uploading your writing and getting feedback: **www.wattpad.com**

Poem Hunter lets young writers upload poems and get feedback: **www.poemhunter.com**

The National Literacy Trust website has information about competitions: **www.literacytrust.org.uk**

The BBC has an annual Young Writers Award: **www.bbc.co.uk/ programmes/articles/4PrGlh3csfFgrgdw43K698Q/the-bbc-young-writers-award-2017** The BBC also runs a short story competition, 500 Words: **www.bbc.co.uk/programmes/articles /13FxbKl0D1DP80zvWRgw2CK/submit-your-500-words-story**

Aspiring authors can find advice about publishing on the Society of Authors website at **www.societyofauthors.org**

For craft, visit Etsy: **www.etsy.com**

Young Film Academy helps young people make and share digital films, both in front of and behind the camera: **www.youngfilmacademy.co.uk**

Reading on Screens

So much of what we read nowadays is on a screen, rather than on paper. There are two sorts of screen-based reading: online and offline. Online is everything we read on the Web via the Internet and all the messages that come to us on our smartphones and other devices, either through Wi-Fi or our mobile signal. Offline is everything we read when we are on a screen that is not connected to the Internet: on eBook readers, or a reading app on our phone or tablet, or when we read text that we have downloaded from the Internet to read later on any of our digital devices.

The evidence is that most of us are reading a *lot*, a lot more than we were before all this digital technology and the Internet. Information scientists have tried to measure this and the figures are astonishing. Bear in mind that all these figures are, obviously, averages, and some people will be reading much more or much less, but according to Daniel J. Levitin in *The Organized Mind*: "In 2011, Americans took in five times as much information every day as they did in 1986 – the equivalent of 175 newspapers. During our leisure time, not counting work, each of us processes 34 gigabytes or 100,000 words every day." In the section

How Big Is It? near the beginning of this book, you saw some of the other statistics that show how much information comes at us every day.

We need to be cautious about these statistics, though. Notice that Levitin doesn't say "read", but "took in" and "processes". Are we really reading all that stuff? Could we read that much in one day? (100,000 words is the length of a large novel.) I think we need a new word for what it is we might be doing with all the words and images coming at us from our screens each day. I haven't thought of that word yet, but I'm working on it!

Let's look at the positives and negatives of reading on screens.

Positives

OPPORTUNITY TO READ MORE AND MORE WIDELY

If you have something to research, there's no doubt that you can find and read many more articles online than if you only had access to physical books and magazines. Researching via the Internet allows you to find, skim, bookmark, discard, screenshot and copy quotes incredibly easily.

I've already talked about the ability to find facts and grow knowledge because of the amount of information out there, but here I'm talking about how the tools on your device allow you to use this material cleverly and efficiently.

ABILITY TO SKIM-READ

Because we are offered so much information, we are likely to be becoming better at "skim-reading": scanning a document with our eyes, picking out the important points and getting the gist of the argument or information quickly. I'll mention in a minute that this may also have a negative side, but I think we can agree that the ability to read something fast and pick out what's important is a useful skill, *if* the article we are reading has good information... Online articles do tend to be written or laid out in a way that makes skimming easy, with bullet points and subheadings, and key words in bold.

FREE OR LOW COST

Of course, almost everything we read online is free. Scientific or other expert journals usually require a subscription but your school may have access to the ones you need, and almost everything has a version that is free.

When it comes to novels or other books that you might read for pleasure on your eBook reader or reading app on your computer, most new eBooks are cheaper than a printed book and many, especially older classics, are free.

When I say "free", I'm obviously ignoring the cost of buying the device you're reading on! And those are certainly *not* free.

COMMUNITY

When you read online, you don't have to be alone. There are communities of people who like the same types of book, author or topic that you do.

Also, if you're reading an article or factual piece, there are often comments from readers showing how they agree or disagree. So if someone has written something wrong or silly or controversial, readers will pick them up on it and you, as a reader, get the chance to see what the flaws in the article might be. Although many comments below articles can be nasty, ignorant and arrogant, you can see the discussions take place and make your own judgement. And sometimes the comments are valid, opening up new views.

For example, I've been helped when I've read a report of a piece of research but then in the comments someone has pointed out that this was a very small study which hasn't been repeated and therefore might not be correct.

ENVIRONMENTALLY FRIENDLY

I should start by saying that none of the electronic devices we read on are exactly environmentally friendly. In fact, the manufacturing process and some of their components, added to the fact that they will usually end up in landfill sites, make them extremely damaging. However, reading things on a screen does mean much less use of paper. You might argue that saving paper is not comparable with the vast amount of waste from the manufacturing of the devices, but on the other hand most of those gadgets are used not only for reading but for many other activities, too. They would be manufactured even if we didn't read on them. So, if you're reading on devices that are multi-purpose, and if you're reading things that otherwise would have been printed, that's an arguable positive.

PEOPLE DON'T KNOW WHAT BOOK YOU'RE READING

There are times when you don't want to be judged on the book you're reading. And people do judge, so it's your right if you decide you just want to keep it private. Maybe you're not confident about reading, so you've chosen a book that's nice and easy but you think people will judge you as not being a good reader. Most writers for young people would agree with me that anyone should feel free to read anything; we often read and enjoy books that were written for teenagers or children or want to read something that others might think too easy or shallow. I understand that you might feel you don't want people to judge your reading ability based on your book choice. An eBook reader or reading on your phone allows you to avoid that.

Or maybe you're reading a book you think adults will disapprove of. Again, while I respect caring adults for wanting to guide your reading, I believe that once you've arrived at adolescence you should feel free to read anything you're interested in and that you enjoy. Teenagers often like to take risks and I'd far rather you took them with your reading choices than in life. One great thing about books (as opposed to films and videos) is that you can stop reading before it gets too scary or unpleasant. In books, there are always clues that something is going to become too much and each reader has the chance to stop.

Please note that I'm only talking about books, not websites. There are certainly websites that can do great harm to people who access them: pornography sites, for example, or sites that encourage anorexic or bulimic behaviour. This harm comes partly because these sites include visual images that may disturb you before you've had a chance to switch off, and partly – mainly – because they have not gone through a responsible, caring editing process to make sure the information and messages are correct, valuable and true.

For books, if we believe that reading choices should be personal, as I do, eBook readers allow privacy and help you explore and enjoy your reading without being judged.

ADAPTABLE FOR YOUR NEEDS

One of the great things about reading on screen is that you can adapt the appearance to make it easier to read. With an eBook reader, you can change the font style and print size and this is extremely helpful for people with some forms of dyslexia or with a whole range of sight problems. Sometimes you can also listen to a voice version, even if there isn't a special audio edition of that book.

WON'T BREAK YOUR BACK!

If you're a keen reader, you can carry as many books as you want without straining your muscles or damaging your bag. Choosing eBooks means you can also avoid carrying lots of books to and from school. Many schools ask students to have tablets, so you have much less to carry around or lose. Or forget. You can pack all your holiday reading easily and if you can't decide which books to take, you can take lots! An eBook reader is so slim and light that it can easily fit into any bag and you've always got reading material with you!

Negatives

Those all sound like useful positives, so let's see how they may be balanced by some possible negatives. There are quite a few studies supporting these but it's worth saying that the research isn't conclusive and we probably need another ten years or more of data before we can be sure if these are significant. I think they make sense, though, and so are worth bearing in mind.

LOSING ABILITY TO READ DEEPLY OR SLOWLY

The brain works on a "use it or lose it" principle. When we practise something, we grow and strengthen connections between neurons; if we carry on doing that activity and therefore using those connections, they stay strong; if we stop doing the activity, the connections weaken and some will die, so we become less good at that activity or skill. And if we never learnt to do the thing in the first place, we obviously won't have the connections.

For example, if you learn the piano, you grow connections in certain areas; the longer you learn and the more you practise, the more and stronger those connections will be. If you then stop practising for a while, when you try to play again, you will notice yourself being out of practice. This is because your connections have become weaker and some may have died.

This is the same with anything, including the skill of focusing on and understanding a difficult piece of reading. We know this is how the brain works.

So, it's likely that if you do lots of skim-reading and much less deep and difficult, focused reading, it will become harder to do that sort of reading. And sometimes deep reading is important.

Recently, I felt I'd become worse at deep reading. I was finding it really hard to concentrate on something difficult, such as text with very long sentences and complicated ideas. So I took matters into my own hands. I cut out from a journal a long and difficult article that I was wanting to understand. I now carry it with me on train or bus journeys and I make myself focus on it for twenty minutes. It's a bit like piano practice, and I'm noticing the improvement. Once I've completely got to grips with that article, I'll find another one, but it's the act of trying to do it that seems to make the difference to my focus and deep reading.

It's possible that people who have grown up entirely in the digital age have done much less deep and focused reading than older people, because a lot of what we used to read at school was written in complex sentences that were designed to be difficult. So much of what we all read now – and this is certainly true for school materials – is designed to be read quickly and skimmed to grasp the main points. So you might be a bit like someone who has only learnt to play simple piano tunes: as a reader, you may not have developed the skills and brain networks to allow or encourage you to focus on a difficult piece of text. But when you get towards the end of school or go to college and university, you will need those skills.

We don't know for certain that we are losing those deep reading skills or that people your age on average have less good deep reading skills than people my age; but it makes sense, based on how brains become better or worse at things and based on the type of reading we are mostly doing; and many teachers say they are noticing this trend. Again, I'm noticing it in myself. And I care about it.

HOW TO AVOID THIS NEGATIVE:

1. Make yourself practise regularly by finding something to read that is difficult or that you don't understand at first. Switch off all distractions and make yourself do it for ten to fifteen minutes. It doesn't matter if you still don't completely understand it: this is just practice. It's the mental exercise that counts. Soon you'll find it easier.

2. When you are reading something important, tell yourself: "I'll read this slowly and concentrate."

3. Take notes with pen and paper, making your own bullet points.

EASY TO MISS THE POINT OR BE DECEIVED

If we are trying to read something as quickly as possible, using our great skim-reading skills and being led by the headings and bullet points, we may miss important facts. We may think we know what the article says but we only know part of it. Many newspaper articles or persuasive pieces are written deliberately to make us believe a certain thing, so the heading will suggest a particular idea and perhaps the first couple of paragraphs will support that; but it may only be towards the end of the article, or hidden away in a particular paragraph, that a really vital piece of evidence is obscured.

For example, a newspaper headline might say: "CHOCOLATE IMPROVES MOOD". And the first paragraph might talk about how scientists have done some research in which eating chocolate raised the mood of participants, suggesting that chocolate is an important part of well-being. Only when you read closely and all the way to the end of the article might you discover that, for example, this was a study on mice, not humans – or perhaps it was on humans but there were only sixteen people in the study and none were suffering from depression; that the amount of chocolate required was so huge it would be very difficult and unhealthy to eat; it had to be chocolate with 80% cocoa solids, which most people would find very unpleasant.

This might sound like an exaggeration but I have seen all of those problems in newspaper articles that seemed to suggest something very dramatic in the headline. I have heard people say things based on headlines where they simply haven't noticed crucial facts from the rest of the article. It's very tempting to believe a headline when we're too busy to read the whole story or when the details of the research aren't there.

HOW TO AVOID THIS NEGATIVE:

1. Simply being aware that what you're reading could be deceiving you should encourage you to read more carefully. No one really wants to be tricked or be ignorant so it's worth taking time to read the whole article and think carefully about it.

2. Challenge what you read. How do the writers know? Why are they saying it? Have they read the research properly? Are they trying to make us believe something?

DISTRACTIONS ON THE SCREEN AND IN THE TEXT

When we read on a screen, there are almost always other things on the screen to distract us. If we are reading from a website, there are icons and maybe adverts on the sidebars, trying to attract our attention. Remember: we are programmed to be distractible so we will tend to notice things at the side of our vision. Even if we manage to ignore them and stay on the task of reading, a part of our attention – our brain bandwidth – is occupied by the distraction and it is then slightly harder to focus on what we're reading.

A great deal of research now shows that almost all of us do lose some concentration and performance when we read on screen with these potential distractions.

Something else that distracts us is the appearance of a hyperlink. When we come to a hyperlink, we have to make a decision: follow the link, in which case we inevitably lose the thread of what we were reading, even if only briefly; or decide not to follow the hyperlink. Whichever we do, we've lost a tiny bit of concentration as we make that decision and even if we ignore the link it takes a bit of time to get back to what we were reading. The hyperlink is tempting because, remember, as well as being programmed to be distractible, we are also programmed to be curious. It might lead to something fascinating and more interesting than what we are reading. Also, resisting temptation occupies a lot of brain bandwidth (and research suggests *more* than following temptation), so *not* clicking on the hyperlink could cost us more attention than we might think.

Also, when we are connected to the Internet, there's a possibility of notifications coming: we might receive an email or social media notification. Even if we ignore them, we've lost a bit of focus. If that happens often, that loss mounts up and means we take longer over the piece of work and may do it less well.

What about eBook readers that aren't connected to the Internet, so there are no hyperlinks and no notifications? There are still some distractions: you find highlighted bits of text that say things like, "178 people also highlighted this area" – and you find yourself wondering, "Ooh, what's so important about this? Why did they highlight this?" And for a few moments it takes you out of your concentration zone, because you're suddenly thinking about other people.

There's even evidence that if you are reading or writing on paper but the person next to you has a screen open, *your* attention suffers. This may be because a little part of you starts to think about your smartphone or the possibility of going on social media. We know that just *thinking* about doing these things gives a rush of dopamine, the excitement chemical.

There's now a lot of research on the effects of reading on screens, and while some of it consists of very small studies and in most cases the results show only a small effect, the effect really does seem to be there. It is worth being aware of. None of this matters much if what you're reading isn't very important. But what if you're trying to learn or understand new things? Trying to do the best work possible? Trying to be the best you can be at your subject? I think it matters.

HOW TO AVOID THIS NEGATIVE:

1. When you read on a screen, do everything you can to remove distractions: switch off social media platforms and your email or anything else that might bring you a message. If you can switch your screen to show only the text and eliminate menus, do so.
2. When reading on screen, use an app to block social media.
3. Don't open hyperlinks until you've finished the article.

COMPREHENSION AND MEMORY

There's a lot of research now into how reading or taking notes digitally compares with reading print or writing by hand. Most studies suggest a small benefit for most people from reading and note-taking with paper and ink. This small difference may not be enough to mean that you should always choose paper, but it's worth knowing. When we read on screen (online or on an eBook reader) we are usually *slightly* less good at comprehension, processing and recall. When we take notes by hand, we tend to process what we're hearing better because we have to find a way to put it in fewer words. This is because handwriting tends to be slower than typing; when we type we are more likely simply to type what we hear, without processing it in our minds.

As I say, this effect is only small, and, as with all such research, it's about averages, and of course some people don't fit the overall findings, so I'm not suggesting that schools should ditch tablets and laptops and only use printed books. However, I would also strongly argue against ditching printed books and only using screens... There's something about paper and ink that helps us concentrate and something about screens that can make that harder. And when a piece of reading is difficult or new to us, I suggest we can't afford to lose even a tiny bit of our focus and ability to grasp meaning.

It's not just the possible distractions from screens, but also aspects of how we learn to read that can make print somewhat easier. Reading is a very complex set of skills and there is no brain area that has evolved specifically "for" reading, as there are areas for seeing, moving, coordination. Reading uses areas which evolved for other activities. So, when we learn to read, we use areas which originally developed for seeing, direction, coordination, understanding, language and hearing, among others. We use our senses of sight and touch. We notice where on the page the text is and how far into the book we are; we hold the book and sense how thick it is; we may trace our fingers over the print while touching the paper.

When we read on screen, we lose those sensations. We don't know where on the page the word was because the page moves; we don't know how far through the book we are by using our sense of touch. We are somewhat disconnected from the words; they are not quite there in front of us for us to touch and hold, but more "out there". All these effects are tiny, but I think they go some way to explain why very many people, including young people who have grown up in a digital world, find it slightly harder to engage fully with the text. We lose something when we read digitally and sometimes – for some people at least – that might be important.

HOW TO AVOID THIS NEGATIVE:

1. Since there's a good chance that reading print will be slightly easier and more effective than reading on screen, if you are reading on screen make an extra effort to read the whole article. Make handwritten notes as you go.

2. With online articles that you really want to concentrate on, download from the Web and either read on an offline screen or print out to study carefully.

READING FOR PLEASURE MAY BE MORE DIFFICULT

I've talked about reading for meaning and understanding, focusing on those times when we are trying to understand something difficult or new. But what about reading for pleasure? It's an activity that plays a really important part in well-being. One reason for its importance is that it's one activity or pastime which encourages us to be in a state of engagement. Engagement is when you are fully "on task", totally immersed, carried away in the experience. Positive psychologists such as Martin Seligman believe that this state of engagement is one of the crucial ingredients of well-being.

But what's wrong with reading for pleasure on a screen? Lots of people love reading eBooks on their Kindles or other eBook readers, don't they?

Yes, they do. And for readers who find it easy to dive into a book when it's on their eBook reader, that's great. There's no way I'd discourage it. If it works for you, fine. But lots of readers also say that they find it harder – some people say only slightly harder, while others find it much harder – to get into an eBook than a printed book. If it's harder to get *into* the book, there's a greater chance of giving up, of not getting to that state of being carried away, of not fully engaging with the book. That phrase "I can't get into the book" is one that's more likely then. And that means people might tend to read less for pleasure and have less of that wonderful state of engagement.

For readers who are not yet confident or who find reading hard work, it's likely to be even harder to reach that state of being fully engaged with the book. (I realize that those readers are also helped in some ways by eBooks, as they can change the font, read what they want, etc., but here I'm talking about the *desire* to read. If the desire is weak in the first place, eBooks are easier to ignore or forget and it's harder to make the necessary effort.)

It seems to me, after looking at all the evidence I can find, that although eBooks bring great benefits, they also make it slightly harder to engage for many people, and much harder for some. Personally, I do find it hard to engage with an eBook, though I wanted to and have tried hard. You might say, "Oh, but that's because you grew up with print so you're not used to digital." But actually the research doesn't suggest an age difference. Young people also, on average, find it harder to escape fully into the story when they are reading on a screen.

But, as I say, if you love reading eBooks and find it easy, don't let me stop you: just read!

HOW TO AVOID THIS NEGATIVE:

1. If you enjoy reading for pleasure, treat this as pleasure that is good for you: give yourself every chance to do it, whether print or digital. I call it "readaxation" because we have good evidence that reading for pleasure is effective for relaxation.

2. If you find that eBooks are harder to get into, choose print books. Use your local library: it's free and you can order any book you like!

3. When you do read for pleasure, notice the benefit it gives you.

Summing Up

The digital reading world allows us to access far, far more than we could have before the Internet and the Web. It's usually free, designed to be easy to read, find, download, use in any way you wish. It's more democratic, in the sense that anyone can give their opinion on the book or article and anyone can argue and have a voice.

But it's not a replacement for print reading. It's an "and" not an "or". If we want to concentrate really well on the text, understand it fully and remember it properly, we will do ourselves a favour by at least sometimes reading on paper. And if we find that we don't *enjoy* our reading for pleasure so much on a screen, we're not alone in that. The solutions are in our hands: choose print or screen to suit your personal needs and wishes.

Resources

"Welcome to the information age – 174 newspapers a day" by Richard Alleyne (2011) can be found at **www.telegraph.co.uk/news/science/science-news/8316534/Welcome-to-the-information-age-174-newspapers-a-day.html**

Roger E. Bohn and James E. Short's report for the Global Information Industry Center – "How Much Information? 2009 Report on American Consumers" – can be read online at **www.researchgate.net/publication/242562463_How_Much_Information_2009_Report_on_American_Consumers**

"Readers absorb less on Kindles than on paper, study finds" by Alison Flood (2014) discusses a study suggesting that plot recall after reading on screen is poorer than reading on paper: **www.theguardian.com/books/2014/aug/19/readers-absorb-less-kindles-paper-study-plot-ereader-digitisation**

Dianna Dilworth's "Reading Print Versus Digital Increases Comprehension: Study" (2014) discusses research that suggests reading on screen might be less effective than reading on paper: **www.mediabistro.com/galleycat/reading-print-versus-digital-increases-comprehension-study_b89129**

Martin Seligman's PERMA well-being model and an explanation of "engagement" are discussed in this 2017 article, "The PERMA Model: Your Scientific Theory of Happiness": **www.positivepsychologyprogram.com/perma-model/#engagement**

My website has many resources on reading and wellbeing: **www.nicolamorgan.com/category/the-reading-brain/** And you can put "readaxation" into the search box for posts specifically about that, including a "readaxation diary" to download.

You can find further discussion of paper versus screens in "What does your brain like better – print or ebooks?" by Dennis Abrams (2014): **www.publishingperspectives.com/2014/06/what-does-your-brain-like-better-paper-or-ebooks/**

"The Reading Brain in the Digital Age: The Science of Paper versus Screens" by Ferris Jabr in *Scientific American Mind* (2013) has more: **www.scientificamerican.com/article/reading-paper-screens/**

Great research was commissioned in 2016 and 2017 by the publisher Egmont. See "Print Matters More" at **www.egmont. co.uk/research/print-matters-more/**

"How distracting are laptops in class?" (2013) by teacher Valerie Strauss discusses research by David Willingham suggesting laptops in class harm the attention even of those not using them: **www.washingtonpost.com/news/answer-sheet/wp/2013/08/20/how-distracting-are-laptops-in-class/**

Find some good tips for minimising distractions when reading on screen in Hacker Noon's "Improving Reading Focus By Dimming Online Distractions": **www.hackernoon.com/improving-reading-focus-by-dimming-online-distractions-ae52726abe1**

The Internet and Mood

This is something people worry about a lot and there's some argument about what the science so far says. Are the Internet and social media good or bad for mental health? Are some people more vulnerable than others? Media headlines most often suggest negatives, and there's some research to back up the concerns. But then you'll find a headline such as "FOUR HOURS OF SCREEN TIME 'AIDS WELL-BEING' OF TEENAGERS", which was reporting on the results of a large survey of fifteen year olds and which found benefits to certain amounts of screen time per day, because young people who are completely cut off from the social benefits of screen time may suffer. In that particular study into what was called the Goldilocks theory, scientists found that well-being was best when the fifteen year olds had no more than slightly over four hours of computer time, about two hours of smartphone time and one hour and forty minutes of video gaming. (Note that those activities might in practice be happening at the same time.) That was just one study and it's a tricky area of research, because some effects are hard to measure and some of the things measured are very specific and may not translate to a whole-life situation.

So, what's going on? What might the benefits and problems be when it comes to mental health, mood and well-being?

Note that there is a bit of overlap with the section **Social Life Online**, but here I'm thinking of mood more generally. You might want to go back there and remind yourself of some of the negatives, though.

Positives

FRIENDSHIP AND WELL-BEING

In **Social Life Online**, I talked about how life online makes it possible to have lots more friends, and to make friends if you're either shy or for practical reasons cut off from possible face-to-face connection. And I explained that having these networks is important to how we function as individuals: we need people to support us. I want to remind you of a particular sentence: "Being excluded or not having good friends and networks is one of the most difficult things for us to deal with – in fact, it's bad for our well-being and mental health..."

So, being able to connect to people online can have a major effect on our happiness and mood. When I've had a hard day, or someone has upset me, or when something wonderful has happened, I want to be able to share this with particular friends. Often I can't do this with one friend, perhaps because I know she's preoccupied with something in her own life, so instead I choose the next most appropriate friend to connect to. You might say, "But you could do that before the Internet; we did have phones, you know!" Yes, but now, with life online, I can do it very easily, to several people at once if necessary, and, crucially, without intruding on them or disturbing what they are doing. Phoning someone is quite a big thing and you need to know someone pretty well before you can phone them and offload your good or bad news. But being able to send a quick text or WhatsApp or Facebook private message is easy for me and, importantly, for them. If they don't have time to answer, they don't have to. But answering may only take a few seconds so they easily can.

Being able to contact a wide range of friends easily, for them and for us, helps our well-being and allows us to react appropriately and quickly to our needs, having an immediate effect on our mood.

SUPPORT

Connected closely to that, when we are going through a really bad phase, we can easily get help. Not just from our friends but from whatever organization is there to help us. People who suffer from mental illnesses such as depression or anxiety disorder, or people who are dealing with a difficult problem or situations such as bereavement, can get expert, instant help without having to wait for an appointment or travel somewhere.

EASY TO FIND THINGS TO MAKE US LAUGH

Laughter is instant medicine. The act of smiling and laughing triggers the brain into producing endorphins, sometimes called nature's happy chemicals. Finding something to make you laugh is one of the simplest pieces of advice I have to raise your mood if you're feeling a bit down. And the Internet – particularly YouTube – is full of opportunities to do that. You'll probably have your own favourites but mine are things like videos of babies eating lemons, goats screaming like humans and dogs talking.

EASY TO FIND THINGS TO ENGAGE THE MIND

Sometimes we want to take our mind off whatever is bothering, annoying or upsetting us. Or just to relax after a hard day at school or work. And, yes, there are masses of things we could do in the offline world – meeting friends, kicking a ball about, going to the cinema, for example – and they're all great things. But sometimes we need something *now*, something quick, something to engage our mind for a few minutes.

I have a couple of games I play on my phone. I can use them if I find my thoughts starting to fixate on negative things. A few minutes on one of those games can take my mind off whatever was bugging me. As long as it's just a few minutes...

Negatives

We are starting to have research into any mental health negatives that may come from life online or from too much time spent on our devices, but we're not yet at the stage where we can be sure exactly how bad the negative effects might be, how easy it is still to have good mental health while spending a lot of time online, and which activities might be more or less risky for mental health. So, while we're waiting for more research, what we have is our instinct and common sense. In any case, we should not live our lives only based on studies and research! As you read these possible negatives, remember that these will affect some people more than others and they might not affect you at all, but that I believe we still should be aware of them.

INCREASED ANXIETY

Remember I said early on in this book that we are programmed to be anxious? I gave the example of a human from thousands of years ago, when our brains first evolved to their current state, hearing that a lion had killed someone in a nearby village. The person would feel very fearful, and that anxiety would keep them alert and therefore safe. When we hear something bad happening nearby, there's a risk it might happen to us.

How does life online make this a problem? Well,

165

thousands of years ago, the only stories we'd hear would be of things happening very close by. So they would be genuinely relevant to our own safety because there'd be a high chance of the same thing happening to us: lion attack, rabid dog on the loose, fever outbreak. But now we hear, over and over and over again, stories of disaster or danger happening elsewhere in the world. It's unlikely that we are going to be affected, so we usually don't need to be anxious and alert, but we feel anxious and alert because our brains are still behaving in an ancient way. We can't stop that happening but we can tell ourselves the truth: that statistically this thing is unlikely to happen to us so we should just carry on with our lives.

This depends, of course, where you live. Some parts of the world are obviously much more dangerous than others, as they may be in the middle of a war or a natural disaster, so sometimes you do genuinely need to be anxious. But let's take the UK, other parts of Europe, the US and Australia. Although all these countries have had terrorist attacks in recent years, which may be making you anxious, you are still statistically incredibly unlikely to be caught up in one.

When we use our phones or go online, we see or hear repeated news stories that make us fearful when we don't actually need to be. And if we feel too worried too often, and we don't process the news in the context of reality, we risk becoming anxious people, or even suffering an anxiety disorder when worry dominates us instead of being a natural, life-saving mechanism.

HOW TO AVOID THIS NEGATIVE:

1. If you know you're vulnerable to anxiety, don't torment yourself by reading bad news stories too much. If something bad has happened in the world, just read the headline and maybe listen to the news story once. Then don't look any more.
2. Disable news alerts on your phone.
3. When you feel anxious and jittery or you have repeated negative thoughts going through your head, practise breathing and relaxation techniques.

BAD NEWS CAN LOWER MOOD

As well as making us anxious, bad news stories can lower our mood, making us feel down. This is a natural human reaction: we hear something sad and we feel a bit sad. It's empathy, and that's a good thing. However, the Web and our use of our smartphones mean there's the potential for hearing sad stories so often that, at least for some people, there can be too much of a downward mood spiral. Also, if you are already suffering low mood or have a tendency to depression, hearing bad news stories can make this worse.

You might be interested to know that when aid workers work in areas of disaster, or when psychologists listen to stories of abuse or tragedy, after a while they often need counselling so that they can process all the negative emotions they inevitably feel.

Research suggests that it probably isn't simply possessing a smartphone that increases unhappiness: it's using it too much. If you're feeling fine, being online shouldn't be a problem. But if you're down or over-anxious, being online more is likely to have a negative effect. Also, when your mood is low, it can be harder to do the sensible thing and avoid negative stories; people often have less willpower when they feel down.

HOW TO AVOID THIS NEGATIVE:

1. Exactly the same as for the previous point: protect yourself from repeated bad news, disable alerts and practise relaxation techniques when you're feeling down.
2. Balance the sad news with some happy news or something that makes you laugh.
3. Try to be very aware of your mood so that you can take preventative steps early.

TOO MUCH HEAD NOISE

I mentioned "continuous partial attention" when I was talking about the distractions that our screens bring us. This is not only a problem because it makes it harder for us to concentrate, but it's also a stressful feeling and therefore affects our mood. If we keep being distracted when we are trying to do something, or if we constantly think there's something else we need to be doing, it makes us agitated, alert, unrelaxed. Dissatisfied. That's alright for short periods of time, or when we need to be alert, but after a while it's mentally exhausting.

I call it head noise. Just too much going on in my head. Information coming in, the need to respond, questions, mental notes of things I need to do, more information, worries. Sometimes we might get so used to this that it just seems normal. But you know that feeling when you turn off all your devices? That's peace! And peace is important, physically and mentally.

HOW TO AVOID THIS NEGATIVE:

1. Simple: when you feel that your mind is overloaded, switch off your device. You'll thank yourself.
2. Make sure you have enough moments in every day when you are not at the mercy of your phone. That time you spend offline will help relax, lighten and strengthen you for when you do go back online.
3. Go for a short walk or just do something else. Any physical activity is great. Anything where you can't keep looking at your phone.
4. Look at my **Six Steps to Online Well-Being** pledge at the end of this book and see if you can use it to keep yourself well and positive online.

EVERYONE'S PERFECT LIVES

I mentioned this in the **Social Life Online** section but it's also extremely relevant to mood: the problem is that most people, most of the time, put their "best things" online. They'll upload their best photos (the selfies they've chosen after a hundred and fifty attempts to find the perfect shot), and updates about their fantastic weekends, holidays, news, birthday meals, new boyfriend or girlfriend. It's the version they want people to see: perfect lives, friends and family. And we look at these "perfect" lives and photos and measure them against our own more ordinary ones. We forget – or fail to realize – that those people also have ordinary lives: they're just showing us the glossy bits. They aren't exactly being deceitful, as it's not deliberate. But it will often lower our mood. And if something bad has just happened to you – such as a relationship break-up – then it can feel really awful, particularly if the person posting the happy messages is the person you've just split up with.

In Donna Freitas's book, *The Happiness Effect*, she quotes a young woman as saying "'people share the best versions of themselves, and we compare that to the worst versions of ourselves'". I think this is a really good way of looking at it. We see someone's great picture and we compare it with how we look when we've just woken up; we see someone's post about their amazing birthday and we remember the bit of ours that wasn't perfect; we see someone gazing into the eyes of the person they love and we can only think of our recently broken relationship or the problems we're having with friends.

Many people tend to judge themselves – and therefore feel good or bad – according to how many people have "liked" their photo, post or status update. If hardly anyone has reacted positively, they tend to be disappointed. For young people, who are trying to become the person they want to be and who particularly need positive feedback, it can be very undermining if people don't "like" what they're doing online. They might start to think they're unpopular, boring, unlikeable.

This sometimes leads people to do "like-spamming", where you click "like" for lots of other people's posts just so that they will "like" yours.

It is perfectly natural behaviour but not good for mood. We want people to like us, of course, but spending too much time worrying about whether they do and whether we deserve approval is not a positive way to live.

Surely we are worth more than a few clicks of the "like" button? We certainly are, but social media encourages us to worry that we aren't.

HOW TO AVOID THIS NEGATIVE:

1. Keep reminding yourself that you are only seeing very selected glimpses of people's lives: only their best sides.
2. If you find that your mood drops when you spend too much time online, switch off, walk away and involve

yourself in something else. It will really help to distract you from your negative state of mind.

3. Online as well as offline, keep away from people and places that make you feel bad.

ANGRY REACTIONS

Before life online, if there was something you were cross about or wanted to complain about, you often couldn't react straight away, unless, of course, you were already face to face with the person you were angry with. You would have had to either find the person or write a letter. Being angry face to face is often a difficult thing to do; we tend to moderate what we say, rightly, because we can see the person's reaction. Writing a letter meant we had to delay – while we wrote it, found an envelope and stamp, walked to the post office and posted it. Also, we were always encouraged to wait till the next day, till our anger had calmed a little, so that we would use our head as well as our heart.

Now we can react instantly, sending an angry text, email or message via social media. In just one small movement of one finger, the message has gone. We can't get it back if we suddenly think perhaps we were too angry, too aggressive, even perhaps offensive. And remember the online disinhibition effect? Because we are responding online, where we can't see the person's reaction, we are likely to be a little less careful, more emotional, less reasonable, less empathetic.

There's nothing wrong with being angry. It's a natural human reaction and sometimes very reasonable and valid. If someone has treated you badly, you're allowed to feel angry. But do you want to overreact or might it be better to take time to think of the best response? Stopping to work out the most appropriate way to respond to someone who has made you angry is surely a good thing? Sometimes we do regret our instant angry responses; sometimes they make the situation worse and make us feel bad. Our Internet-connected devices give us the possibility to respond instantly, without being face to face, without thinking. And that's hard to resist. We need a lot of self-control, and emotions get in the way of that.

HOW TO AVOID THIS NEGATIVE:

1. Remind yourself, often, that an instant angry response is one you may well regret. When you feel angry or emotional, tell yourself to take a few breaths, walk away, and wait until you can think as well as feel. Our feelings always calm down after a while.
2. When someone reacts angrily to you, tell yourself the same thing. They may well be regretting it already. Don't respond. Silence is a brilliant weapon.

Summing Up

Although being online gives us lots of opportunities to have fun and be happy, and to get support from friends and contacts when we're down, the act of being online a lot could create problems for our mental and emotional well-being, our self-esteem and judgement of ourselves. Research into the exact effects of different sorts of screen time on different groups of people is not strong enough to give us clear guidelines about how much is a healthy or safe amount, and any guidelines you read are only guesses. But I don't think we need guidelines like that; we just need to notice how we feel and take sensible steps to walk away when necessary. I notice how much better my well-being is when I've spent what feels like the right amount of time online, and with the right people. I think it's common sense and a valid way to take care of ourselves: to notice our emotions and reactions and act accordingly. We need to be aware of the possibilities of a negative effect on our mood and take sensible steps to keep ourselves healthy. Listen to your body and mind and walk away from harm.

Resources

"A Large-Scale Test of the Goldilocks Hypothesis Quantifying the Relations Between Digital-Screen Use and the Mental Well-Being of Adolescents" by Andrew K. Przybylski and Netta Weinstein (2017) is the study suggesting that a certain amount of screen-time is positive for wellbeing and that having *no* screen time has a negative effect, as might having too much. I mentioned it earlier but here are the two places where you can read about it: **www.myscience.org/news/2017/ moderate_amounts_of_screen_time_may_not_be_bad_for_ teenagers_well_being-2017-oxford** and **www.bigthink.com/ david-ryan-polgar/is-screen-time-bad-for-kids-researchers-find-the-positive-sweet-spot**

Research suggests that it's not *having* a smartphone that increases unhappiness but how much you use it. Again, this is research I've referenced earlier - "Media Use, Face-to-Face Communication, Media Multitasking and Social Well-Being Among 8-12-Year-Old Girls" by Roy Pea, Clifford Nass, Lyn Meheula et al (2012): **www.researchgate. net/publication/221769567_Media_Use_Face-to-Face_ Communication_Media_Multitasking_and_Social_Well-Being_ Among_8-_to_12-Year-Old_Girls**

The full title of Donna Freitas's 2017 book is *The Happiness Effect: How Social Media Is Driving a Generation to Appear Perfect at Any Cost.*

The Internet and Sleep

Sleep is incredibly important to our physical health and mental well-being and also to our ability to learn things. Sleep science is a fascinating area and scientists are discovering more and more about what happens to us and our brains and bodies while we sleep. There's still a lot to discover but what has been learnt in the last few years is extremely important and revealing. We used to think that sleep was just about restoring energy but now we know it's about so much more.

While we are asleep, our brain clears away the rubbish of broken connections or cells, literally washing it away with cerebrospinal fluid. Growth hormone is activated, and much of your growing happens while you're asleep. Hormones that control appetite also depend on good sleep patterns: people who don't have enough sleep tend to eat more during the day, craving sugary foods and carbohydrates. While we sleep our brains process things we were learning during the day, storing the information in the correct brain areas so that we can recall it more easily when we need to. Emotional events of the day are also correctly processed during certain stages of sleep, helping us not be negatively affected by them. And, as we've known for a long time, cells in our body repair during sleep.

During the night, we have five or six cycles of sleep, each about an hour and a half long. In every cycle, there are five different stages or levels of sleep. Stage 1 is short and light. We can have creative insights during this time, and some artists have deliberately tried to wake themselves during this stage so that they can use the ideas that come to them. Stage 2 is also fairly light. It lasts about twenty minutes during the early parts of the night but less in later parts. This is a restful stage. Scientists believe this stage is most important for strengthening brain connections for physical skills such as music and sport. Things that you have to learn "how to do".

Stages 3 and 4 are deeper, and our body is very relaxed. It's difficult to wake during these stages and if we do we will feel groggy and disorientated. It's during this time that our body produces growth hormone, which isn't just for growing but also for repairing cells. In these stages our brain rehearses what we were learning or doing during the day. For example, perhaps we were practising the piano or a dance routine and we kept getting it wrong, or we were trying to learn some German vocab; while we're in deep sleep, our brain will repeat those mental processes and even clean up faulty brain networks.

Stage 5 is when we dream. During this time, our brain is highly active but our body is paralysed. That's why even though we might be having really active dreams, we don't generally act them out physically. Scientists believe that this dreaming stage is important to mental well-being, helping us process traumatic events.

HOW MUCH SLEEP DO WE NEED?

Everyone's a bit different so any figures you read are averages. You might need more than other people or you might function really well on a bit less. Generally, adults need around eight hours and teenagers need just over nine – technically nine and a quarter as an average.

What do the Internet and our smartphone use have to do with sleep? Let's look at the positives and negatives.

Positives

There are no positives! Well, I suppose the fact that you can do an online search for "How to have better sleep" is a positive. But other than that, I'm afraid I think there are really only negatives.

Negatives

All the evidence I've seen points to the fact that people in countries such as the US and the UK have less sleep on average than they did twenty years ago. And some people – particularly younger people – have much less.

The fact that this lessening of sleep and our use of the Internet and smartphones have coincided *doesn't prove* that they are the cause, though. But there are some facts we do know about our use of smartphones and other Internet-connected devices that can lead us to conclude that they often do have a negative effect on sleep.

SCREENS MIMIC DAYLIGHT

Daylight is different from normal artificial light, such as that from your bedroom lights. The part of our brain responsible for switching on and off the sleep hormone, melatonin, partly reacts to daylight. So when it begins to get dark outside (and usually inside), that's a signal for melatonin to switch on. Even if we have electric lights on, especially fairly dim ones, our brain still detects that it's getting towards night-time. There are some other factors, too, such as habit, meals and our age.

Our smartphones, tablets and laptops all emit light that is similar to daylight, rather than electric light. If it's night-time and daylight has stopped coming to your eyes but you are still using a daylight-producing device, your brain can "think" it's still daytime and may not switch on the sleep hormone, so you won't feel sleepy.

Some experts say that you would have to look at your screens a *lot* before this would have an effect. But others say that the effect is worth considering if you want to have better sleep or get to sleep more quickly. And some say that actually just a bit of this daylight would be enough to confuse the body clock, the tiny area of brain that switches melatonin on and off.

MAKES US EXCITED AND ALERT

Even if the daylight is not a factor, it's certainly true that what we read on our screens is likely to make us excited and alert, rather than relaxed, sleepy and winding down. If we are reading information, our brains are alert, ready to absorb it. If we are looking at our screens for entertainment, watching a video, playing games, having a laugh with friends, writing a blog post, creating a social media status update, all those things make our mind wakeful, excited, emotional (whether positively or negatively). None of these things are necessarily bad or unhealthy but they aren't likely to help us relax and feel sleepy.

Also, once we've sent a message of any sort, we are likely to be thinking about the possible reply, and that's not relaxing.

STRESSFUL MESSAGES

Many of the messages we receive on our devices are very stressful. They may be continuing or starting an argument, telling us bad news, or for some reason be irritating, upsetting or stressful. Our heart rate rises and we immediately become less likely to sleep. The message can trigger a spiral of worry which makes sleep seem very far away.

HOW TO AVOID THESE NEGATIVES:

1. Make a strict rule for yourself that you will turn off your phone and all backlit, message-enabled devices at least one and a half hours before you want to start feeling sleepy.

2. Turning devices off may not be enough: put them where you can't see or access them, ideally not even in your bedroom.

3. Never have your phone on while you are asleep. You do not need it for your alarm; you can buy a cheap alarm clock which will do the job perfectly. Don't just have the phone on silent; it needs to be off.

4. Help each other. I strongly recommend that everyone in your household follows exactly the same rule. Yes, parents, too. Everyone needs good sleep and there is absolutely no reason why teenagers and children should have to switch phones off for the sake of their well-being if adults don't.

Summing Up

Sleep is extremely important for physical and mental health and well-being. We know that very many people in countries where smartphones are used a lot are not getting enough sleep, and we know that many people use their devices while they are about to go to sleep and often keep them on throughout the night, too. We know that there are things about these devices that are likely to keep us awake rather than letting us fall asleep quickly. So, we need to act in our own interests and take control by switching off an hour and a half before bedtime. This may be the most important change you make after reading this book.

Resources

"Teens' night-time use of social media 'risks harming mental health'" by Sally Wheale (2015) discusses how night-time use of social media can harm sleep: **www.theguardian.com/society/2015/sep/11/teens-social-media-night-risk-harm-mental-health-research**

"Association Between Portable Screen-Based Media Device Access or Use and Sleep Outcomes" by Ben Carter, Philippa Rees, Lauren Hale et al. (2016) looks at how use of a screen-based device harms sleep quality and quantity: **www.jamanetwork.com/journals/jamapediatrics/article-abstract/2571467**

"Scary ways technology affects your sleep" is a simple and clear article from the National Sleep Foundation: **www.sleep.org/articles/ways-technology-affects-sleep/**

You'll find more detail and science from the Sleep Health Foundation in the fact sheet "Technology and Sleep": **www.sleephealthfoundation.org.au/public-information/fact-sheets-a-z/802-technology-sleep.html**

There's an excellent idea called "Digital Sunset", which I wrote about in "Digital Sunset - a great idea for well-being and sleep" at **www.nicolamorgan.com/life-online/digital-sunset-great-idea-wellbeing-sleep/** You'll find links to a video and a downloadable booklet.

In case you need to be convinced about the importance of sleep, try Matthew Walker's 2017 book, *Why We Sleep: The New Science of Sleep and Dreams*.

Or if you'd lust like to learn about what sleep is, what it's for and how to sleep better, *Night School: Wake Up to the Power of Sleep* by Richard Wiseman (2014) is very comprehensive and readable.

Use Your New Powers

What do you think about what you've read? Was there something that seemed particularly relevant to you? Anything you'd like to change in your online habits? Anything you want to tell your friends or adults about? I have a 23-year-old research assistant who is an expert in social media, and when she was reading the research for this book she decided to change some of her habits immediately. She deleted Facebook from her phone and gave herself strict rules for how and when she would look at her social media. She noticed the benefits.

I've done the same. So much of my work involves being online; so much of my research uses the Internet; and a lot of an author's work nowadays involves connecting with many strangers on social media. And I love it! But I know that when I do it too much, my concentration, my engagement and even my enjoyment of my work decrease while my stress increases. So I take active steps to get offline often enough. When I do that, I really notice how much better I feel and how much easier it is to concentrate. I love to be connected but I also love and need to be disconnected.

And that is in my hands. I think your online life can be

in your hands, too, and I believe you'll notice the benefits if you keep or take back control and build healthy habits. I believe it will help how you feel and how well your brain works; I believe it will boost your well-being.

Tips for Good Screen Habits

There are lots of strategies that will help us, at any age, learn to control our smartphone and any other device use and have a healthy relationship with our devices. Many of these strategies are based on how we treat people with all sorts of addiction, because this is all about habits: breaking bad ones and creating good ones.

- Set yourself a clear goal. For example: "I will work for 25 minutes without looking at my smartphone or checking social media." Use a timer to tell you when your 25 minutes is up. After that allow yourself five minutes on social media before going back to what you were doing for another 25 minutes. The reason I say 25 minutes is based on the Pomodoro technique, which recommends that amount of time because it's easy to stick to, but you can choose any amount of time. Personally, I do 45 minutes because I can get a lot of work done in that time. It's a clever technique because you will often find that when your alarm goes, you're so engrossed in your work that you want to carry on.

It's a brilliant feeling! (But you do need a break at some point.) Another clear goal might be: "I will not look at my phone in the morning until I'm dressed and ready." Or: "I will not look at my phone on the bus home." Use the time to think or listen to music instead, or watch the scenery.

- When you are doing a piece of work or need to focus, put your devices where you can't see them and ideally can't get at them. Out of sight, out of mind. If you have to use a device for work, disable notifications and don't open social media apps.

- Create an "if/then" rule. This was developed by Walter Mischel, who oversaw the well-known "marshmallow tests" looking at self-control and postponing pleasure. Say to yourself, for example, "IF I am tempted to look at my phone in the next 25 minutes, THEN I will take a sip of water instead." Simple but effective! That act of doing something else can break the moment of temptation. And drinking a sip of water is usually a good idea anyway. Double win! (Check out the Digital Sunset Challenge.)

- Make a pact with your friends – or one or two of them – that you will all have a "Switch Off Screen" time each evening, say after 9.30 p.m. Collaborating with friends on reducing your usage is the best way – it's tough doing it alone, especially if you're thinking about them being online without you.

- Make a pact with your family that you will ALL put your phones on the landing or in the hall at a certain time at night and none of you will look at them till morning.
- Get one of the various free apps that measure how much you check your phone: it might shock you! But these apps can be very empowering, too.
- Aim to reduce your usage gradually, rather than all at once.
- Get one of the apps you can set to prevent access to social media for a certain time. Lots of writers I know do this – we need it!
- Consider my **Six Steps to Online Well-Being** pledge. It's a set of promises I think will help us have a good life online. Or make a better set for yourself – you don't have to use mine. Maybe discuss it with your friends, class or family.

SIX STEPS TO ONLINE WELL-BEING

1. I will remember that I am worth more than how many people "like" my posts.
2. I will spend plenty of time talking and listening face to face, too.
3. I will notice when being online is harming me and I will switch off.
4. I will make enough time for healthy sleep and physical exercise.
5. I will make time and space to think, breathe and dream.
6. If I need help, I will ask someone I trust.

The online world is full of enormous, wonderful opportunities to know, create, share, learn, love, discover, perform, help and grow; to be who we want to be; to know who we want to know. Let's use this amazing tool to make the world and our part of it a better place. Let's understand it and take control of it – beginning with one finger, which is all we need to turn it on or off – so that we can truly have a healthy, exciting and positive life online. Rule your devices – don't let them rule you!

Index

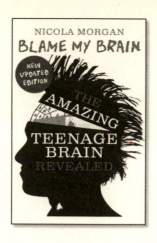

Blame My Brain

Shortlisted for the Aventis prize for science-writing

Scientific research shows what parents have long suspected – the teenage brain IS special! Find out how in this ground-breaking, reassuring and hugely enjoyable book.

From taking risks to sleeping late and depression, uncontrollable emotions to the effects of drugs and alcohol, *Blame My Brain* tells you everything you need to know about the biology and psychology behind the behaviour. Essential reading for teenagers – and parents.

"This is a good resource to share with students to help them deal with what is potentially the most challenging, but also the most exciting, period in their development."
The Times Educational Supplement

The Teenage Guide to Stress

Winner of the School Library Association Award 2015, with both the judges' and readers' awards

Being a teenager can be incredibly stressful. The pressure of exams, changing bodies, social media, bullying and relationships can lead to low self-esteem, depression, anxiety and ill health. *The Teenage Guide to Stress* examines all these problems and more, with great strategies for beating them.

This detailed and sympathetic book reassures teenagers – and the adults who care about them – that they are not alone. And that they CAN beat stress.

"A fantastic self-help book... Just the process of reading this book is cathartic but the guidance provided is wonderful." *Guardian*

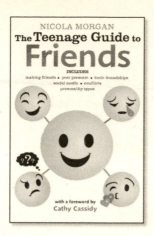

The Teenage Guide to Friends

Friendships and peer groups can cause problems and upsets in your teenage years. People can be confusing – until you understand how different personality traits, stresses and emotions affect behaviour. Yours, too!

The Teenage Guide to Friends is for anyone who wants to know how friendships work, and what to do when they don't. In this book you'll find advice on how to make and keep friends, as well as positive strategies to help you through the tough times and make you feel more confident.

"Nicola Morgan has that rare gift of being able to communicate science and make it fun."
Professor Simon Baron-Cohen, University of Cambridge

Enjoyed *The Teenage Guide to Life Online*?
We'd love to hear your thoughts!

@nicolamorgan
@WalkerBooksUK @WalkerBooksYA

@WalkerBooksYA

Nicola Morgan's website has articles and resources
on many aspects of adolescence, wellbeing and stress
management, the reading brain and life online.
She shares her expertise at events for schools,
festivals and conferences all over the world.
Do visit her website: **www.nicolamorgan.com**